The Naturalist's Guide
to the
BRITISH COASTLINE

The Naturalist's Guide
to the
BRITISH COASTLINE

Ron Freethy

DAVID & CHARLES
Newton Abbot   London   North Pomfret (Vt)

Line illustrations by Carol Pugh

British Library Cataloguing in Publication Data

Freethy, Ron
    The naturalist's guide to the British coastline.
    1. Seashore biology – Great Britain
    I. Title
    500′.941   QH95.7

ISBN 0–7153–8342–6

Filmset in 10 on 12 point Monophoto Century Schoolbook by
Latimer Trend & Company Ltd, Plymouth
and printed in Great Britain
by Butler & Tanner Limited, Frome and London
for David & Charles (Publishers) Limited
Brunel House   Newton Abbot   Devon

Published in the United States of America
by David & Charles Inc
North Pomfret   Vermont 05053   USA

Contents

Introduction

My earliest recollection is of a hot afternoon on a sand dune and the mingling sounds of birds and incoming tide. At the start of Hitler's war a bomb on our street in the shipbuilding town of Barrow had necessitated a return to my mother's native village of Askam-in-Furness, then in the county of Lancashire but now since 1974 part of the new county of Cumbria. An old house was bought in 1941 as a temporary dwelling but such was the beauty of the shore it overlooked that my parents are still there.

As a young naturalist I quickly learned that in the spring the natterjack toads called from the dune slacks, in summer little terns dived into the shallow sea and breeding ringed plovers ran along the stones of the shingle. Here too were the black and red burnet moths, and the heavy droning bumble bees which sucked their fill of the nectar-rich and sweetly scented flowers. As summer gave way to autumn, cockles could be gathered low on the shore and plaice hooked on rod or pre-baited line. As childhood merged into romantic adolescence the deep red sunsets over a backdrop of shimmering sea and purple mountains added an aesthetic overtone to the excited tune of youth. All my friends knew that the saltmarshes provided food for some species of bird, sand dunes for others, while the terns and the sea ducks fished successfully in the bay. On the marshes were finches feeding on the seeds of sea aster, milkwort, thrift, plantain and purslane; in the deep, muddy, tidal gullies, filled with swirling eddies and dangerous currents twice a day due to the gravitational attraction of the moon, redshanks and herons waded patiently. Gradually I was allowed to wander the beaches at night and discover a whole new world of nightlife. Curlews, lapwings and oyster-catchers fed under the cold pale light of a winter's moon, greylag geese called anxiously as they sensed the squelch of my still-distant steps. On an icy night in February, as I approached a mussel bed I heard an unfamiliar crunching sound; peeping round a seaweed-strewn rock I saw, outlined in moonlight, an otter enjoying his supper. On another unforgettable night I counted over two hundred geese as they flew across the yellow disc of a late September moon.

A love like this is never lost and nor does it ever fade; this book is but part of an on-going relationship. It has taken me around the coastline of Britain, allowed me to sit among seabird cities, almost compelled me to look under seaweeds, gaze down into rock-pools and fill countless notebooks with exciting new (to me) knowledge. Therefore it is more true to say that this book compelled me to write it than that any conscious decision was made on my part.

Although the British coastline shows great variety it is perhaps the grandeur of the sea cliffs that creates the most lasting impressions among our visitors. My first chapter therefore concentrates on the natural history of this habitat. The strict geologist may find fault with my classification of cliff systems, but it does, I feel, meet the somewhat different requirements of the naturalist. As many of our most impressive cliffs occur on islands – such as the Western Isles, St Kilda, Handa, the Farnes and the Welsh islands – Chapter 1 does impinge a little upon Chapter 8, where the way in which sub-species develop on islands, as a result of geographical isolation, is the main theme. Chapter 2 deals with our estuaries and the threats they face, and the extensive saltmarshes that often develop alongside estuaries are described in Chapter 3. Chapter 4 considers life forms which can exist among the inhospitable rolling pebbles of a shingle beach, and Chapter 5 describes the way a sand dune can develop from an open beach or from a shingle beach. Holidaymakers funnel into these heat traps to sunbathe while the naturalists, young and old, look hard into the rock-pools in search of an incredible assortment of life-forms. A few of these are described in Chapter 7, although it was hard in this chapter, as in all the others, to do justice to the great variety of life.

This may read as if wildlife carries on oblivious to human activities, but Chapter 9 considers the coastline and industry. The ardent conservationist may find fault with my tendency to consider the good done by oil companies, the Atomic Energy Authority and British Gas, but we must be realistic. We need fuel to survive and we need plastics and chemicals. Many industries are concerned about the environment and are spending large sums of money to limit the potentially devastating effect of their activities. The job of the naturalist is to keep up the pressure for even more care to be taken rather than to try to ban an industry altogether. My optimism was not dampened as I drove my car around the coastline in order to research 101 special places to see, an admittedly personal gazetteer.

I must have omitted to mention many areas of outstanding beauty and scientific significance, and would be more than pleased to have readers' views and look forward to visiting areas at present unknown to me, of which there must be many.

1
Sea Cliffs

There is no finer experience to a naturalist than sailing in a small boat beneath a towering sea cliff. The sound of the inhabitants of a seabird city squabbling over territory remains forever in the memory, as does the often overpowering stench of ammonia-based guano which showers down from flying birds like a winter snow-storm. Man has known for centuries of the value of guano as a rich fertiliser. To sail alongside the cliffs is one thing, but to land and scramble up and along the rocks and slopes, dripping with slippery guano and treacherous with seaweed, is another. Many of Britain's cliffs cannot and should not be climbed, but modern telescopes, binoculars and telephoto lenses allow excellent views of eggs and birds. These are often delightfully surrounded by tufts of golden samphire, its gilded flowers contrasting pleasantly with the succulent green of the leaves, thrift, sea campion, stonecrop and sea plantain. Climb on to the grass verges (carefully!) still within sight and sound of the wheeling birds, but with the heady stench of their droppings muted by the sweet odour of bird's-foot trefoil, kidney vetch, sea storksbill, vernal squill, ribwort plantain and thyme, with many other species according to the season.

Any farmer, gardener or naturalist worth his salt knows that the vegetation depends to a great extent on the make-up of the underlying rock, and that the quantity and quality of the plant life determines the animal life of the area. The geology of the British coastline cliffs is magnificently varied and a circular tour affords splendid glimpses of grey limestone, red sandstone, white chalk, hard granite, soft clay, sand and towering columns of basalt. Many hardy life-forms are common to all cliffs, but some species show a distinct preference for one type in particular. Physical factors such as spray, wind and wave, as well as local geology, play their part in the scheme of things.

Limestone Cliffs

Limestone was formed in the days of the shallow seas of cretaceous times some 100 million years ago, and is a sedimentary rock formed

9

Spring squill, a native bulb (E. C. M. Haes)   *Deadly nightshade*

mainly from the shells of molluscs which once abounded in the tepid waters. Chemists know that if dilute acid is dropped on limestone it will fizz and eventually dissolve. The atmosphere contains some 0.03% of carbon-dioxide gas which dissolves slowly in water and therefore the rain which falls is really dilute carbonic acid. This, assisted on the coast by the strength of the sea, gradually breaks down the limestone, and in time caves for seals, crevices for flowers, blowholes to astound human tourists and breeding ledges for birds are created. Limestone cliffs are found at Tenby in South Wales, Llandudno's Great Orme in North Wales, Humphrey Head and Arnside Knott on the Lancashire-Cumbria border, Durness in Scotland and also along the coast of Durham. Limestone is a suitable habitat for flowers, including bloody cranesbill, bird's-foot trefoil, black medick, milkwort, rockrose, dropwort and fascinating deadly nightshade. Some limestone was also laid down in carboniferous times.

Deadly Beauty
Deadly nightshade is a dangerous plant, as children can get a false sense of security when they watch the birds eating the berries and rabbits

chomping away at the foliage. To humans, every part of the plant is dangerous, containing two alkaloid poisons, atropine and hyoscyamine. The vernacular name belladonna – beautiful lady – comes from the use of extracts from the plant to dilate the pupils of the eye: despite the attendant dangers it was often used as a beauty aid by girls anxious to please their lovers. Monks used controlled doses for the relief of pain, and the present distribution of the plant, especially in northern parts, is often the result of medieval ecclesiastical gardening. Furness Abbey, for example, is sited in a valley known as the Vale of the Deadly Nightshade, and Arnside, too, is close to an old priory at Cartmel, still used as the parish church.

Belladonna grows from a perennial underground rhizome; each summer the shoot may reach a height of 1.5m (nearly 5ft). The leaves are arranged in opposite pairs, but have the unique feature that one leaf is much larger than the other. The bell-shaped, glossy reddish-purple flowers are carried on curved, thick, viscid stems, often short. The surface of the petals is prominently veined. Like the flowers, the intensely shining black fruits are sticky to the touch: devil's cherries is a good old name for them, and the Danish name *dwale*, foolish, is also appropriate. Sub-lethal doses of belladonna induce foolish behaviour, and it is now thought that silly old women (and the occasional man) who believed themselves to be witches would mix belladonna with animal fat, probably rendered from a badger carcase – or even in extreme cases, so it was alleged, from the body of a freshly killed human baby – and rubbed the 'flying ointment' on their skin. Recent biochemical research has shown that the fat would make the skin more porous and allow the atropine and hyoscyamine to reach the bloodstream. The effect is to produce nausea and a feeling somewhat like that of floating in the air, with no feeling of contact with terra firma. This is probably how those involved in the black arts became convinced of their supernatural powers.

Other soluble chemicals in addition to calcium carbonate are often found in limestone, and in many parts of the country springs of mineral water have been sought out by those seeking health, whether spiritual or physical – firstly by pilgrims and then by tourists.

Many of these springs are situated inland but some have been associated with sea cliffs, including the appropriately named Holy Well at the foot of Humphrey Head, which was well known to the monks of the nearby Cartmel Priory and there is thought to have been another well on Arnside Knott. It is not only humans who can benefit from the high concentration of salts in these limestone areas. The mollusc populations are usually abundant, due to the high level of calcium salts which they build into their shells. One of the commonest is the banded snail (*Candidula intersecta*), a species also found on chalk cliffs.

Chalk Cliffs

Chalk is really a very pure but comparatively soft form of limestone, and deposits of it are rich in fossils, including those of sea urchins. But the bulk is composed of tiny but fascinating marine creatures called foramenifera. These are protozoan animals with a shell, they are found on many beaches but also are the main constituents of the muddy substrate of deep-sea bottoms. Chalk cliffs are commonly associated with southern England, especially Kent, Sussex, the Isle of Wight and Dorset. The tops of these cliffs, happily often criss-crossed by footpaths, are a riot of summer colour as the chalk downland flora comes into bloom. The sheer variety of species is perhaps even more impressive than the permutation of colour.

The 160m (500ft) of Beachy Head for example abounds with rock samphire (*Crithmum maritimum*), an edible plant mentioned more than once by Shakespeare, the most significant reference being in King Lear. The word samphire originates from the French *sampere*, a diminutive of 'herb de Saint Pierre', the herb of the fisherman who was the rock on which the church was founded. Here then was his flower growing out of the rock. Many of the old herbalists describe the dangers faced by the samphire gatherers hanging from ropes. The flower was used in salads and pickles, and as a treatment for gallstones as well as kidney and bladder complaints. Also found on Beachy Head is black knapweed, dwarf centaury, gorse, small scabious and slender-headed thistle, these being a mere fraction of the list.

Culver Point, Isle of Wight, is also of great interest to the botanist, who may find here field bugloss, yellow sea poppy and pyramidal orchid. The Isle of Wight beckons the flower hunter to the cliff tops near Ventnor. Here the pale chalk cliffs are illuminated by splashes of colour from pink thrift, samphire and sea beet, which is the wild ancestor of both beetroot and sugar beet.

Alexanders

Alexanders (*Smyrnium olusatrum*) is a most interesting member of the umbelliferae, a family which never gives up its secrets easily – it is often difficult to tell one species from another, and in such cases it is best to study the more easily recognisable species so that these may be eliminated when doubt arises. But alexanders is easily recognised and is seldom found more than a stone's-throw from the sea. It is a common plant in the Mediterranean, though only in certain parts of the British Isles such as the south and west does it ever become even locally abundant. It was at one time eaten as a vegetable – just as we crunch celery – and so it is hard to establish for certain whether it is a native or introduced species. Alexanders is a biennial plant (like carrot, another umbellifer) and can reach a height of almost a metre (3ft); its large shiny leaves are divided into leaflets and then subdivided still further into trefoils. The flowers are greeny-yellow and the fruits black and ridged. Most of the umbellifers in Britain flower very late in spring or early in summer, but alexanders often bloom as early as April, which seems to support the contention that the species originated in warmer climates. The old herbalists strengthen this view since they called it *petroselinum Alexandrinum*, the 'parsley from Alexandria'. Again the plant was cultivated in monastery gardens and in his herbal of 1562 Turner recorded the species as growing on Steep Holm in the Bristol Channel, where there had once been a religious house.

Before leaving the white cliffs of England we must make a literary trek to the north of England; to quote Arthur Mee, 'the wall of glistening chalk formed by Speeton, Buckton and Bempton Cliffs comes to an end at Flamborough Head'. Botanically the area is impressive, especially in early summer when the cliffs seem to blaze with flowering gorse, but it is the ornithologists who congregate here, because of the hordes of breeding seabirds including puffins, guillemots, razorbills and kittiwakes; there is an expanding colony of over 100 pairs of gannets, their only breeding site on mainland England. The area is now administered by the RSPB who are doing their usual professional job.

Life has not always been so peaceful for the seabirds around Flamborough, for apart from a group of professional 'eggers' known locally as the 'climmers', up to the year 1880 they also had to face assault from the sea. At this time it was possible to hire a boat and steam around the cliffs shooting the birds off their ledges. By all accounts the 'gun boats' were followed by others which gathered up the dead birds and plucked them of their feathers, which were sold either to the millinery trade or to firms that stuffed cushions and pillows. The modern naturalist sailing these waters can easily see the effect of the sea industriously eroding away at the soft rock, forming the inlets and coves so beloved of the edible crab (*Cancer pagurus*) and therefore the fishermen who hunt it. Many more centuries of wave bashing have been required to produce similar fissures in the much harder sandstone.

Sandstone Cliffs

Although red sandstone is less prone to erosion, nothing can withstand the mighty and regular pulses of the sea for ever, and they gradually widen the bedding planes in the rock and in time produce stacks, blow-holes, arches, gullies, and the ledges and sheltered inlets which are so attractive to plants and animals. Pembrokeshire and Caithness have impressive formations, and at Arbroath and St Bees Head the naturalist is assured of an interesting welcome. The Scottish Wildlife Trust administer a three-mile trail along the Arbroath cliffs beginning at the promenade car park.

Although the whole stretch is basically sandstone, some areas are studded with conglomerates of pebbles and have veins of crystalline calcite and barytes; lime is also much in evidence, helping to support healthy growths of primrose, wood vetch, red campion, meadow cranesbill, greater knapweed, kidney vetch and the attractive blue clustered bell-flower. All this succulent vegetation provides ample nectar for adult lepidoptera and greenery for their larvae. Green-veined white butterflies, small heaths, meadow browns and, especially, common blues abound here.

Common Blue Butterfly
Often accurately referred to as the small blue, the common blue (*Polyommatus icarus*) is one of Britain's most attractive butterflies, and well illustrates what scientists term sexual dimorphism, the male and female being quite different in appearance. It is the male which is blue, the female being basically brown but with some orange spotting, particularly evident on the wings. As in most butterflies the true colours of the blue are best seen when the wings are folded over the back, when only the grey-brown colour spotted with white, black and orange can be seen. This is good camouflage and when the butterfly does open its wings they give a potentially frightening flash of colour. This may distract a predator for just long enough to allow the butterfly to escape. The larvae of the common blue are able to feed upon many species of the pea family, which abound on the cliffs, and several broods may be raised in a good year. Walking the Arbroath cliff tops one July, I found that the extensive growths of ragwort and knapweed were almost weighted down by mating six-spot burnet moths (*Zygaena filipendulae*), a species which is also common in sand-dune systems (see Chapter 5).

Cliff Birds
Arbroath's cliffs provide the natural breeding habitat for two white-rumped but otherwise contrasting species of bird. The house martin (*Delichon urbica*) would be more accurately named the cliff martin. It was thriving long before the houses of civilised man were available, although there can be little doubt that it is one of the species that have benefited from human civilisation: suitable cliff nesting sites must have been at a premium. From April until September the martins sweep into their nest holes in the red cliffs and hawk for flying insects along the beach and grassy slopes. Rock doves (*Columba livia*), the wild ancestors of domestic pigeons, stand on their ledges, but it can be difficult to

St Bees Head, Cumbria (English Tourist Board)

decide whether a particular individual is a pure rock dove or an avian mongrel. The true wild rock dove has two black wing bars and also a prominent white rump. They are becoming rarer, but can still be seen regularly at Arbroath and St Bees.

St Bees Head in Cumbria is the nearest point on mainland Britain to the Isle of Man, and is now a reserve, like Bempton, quietly managed by the RSPB. Seven species of seabird breed on the 100m (300ft) cliffs, herring gull, kittiwake, fulmar, black guillemot, puffin, cormorant and razorbill with a total population of some 5,000 pairs. Although not large as seabird cities go, this is nevertheless an impressive sight on a Cumbrian coastline with few cliffs. At any time of year the cliffs are ideal for those who enjoy seawatching through binoculars or telescopes. The rewards for the patient can often be gannets, Manx shearwaters, red-throated divers, great skuas, or large rafts of assorted wildfowl taking their ease on the waters of the Irish Sea. I always approach these cliffs from the cosy settlement of St Bees and spend some time exploring Fleswick Bay, being careful not to be cut off by the sea. All coastal-based naturalists need up-to-date copies of tide tables (which may be purchased from all seaport chandlers' shops and at most fishing-tackle shops).

For the black guillemot, St Bees Head is the only English breeding station. The tystie, as those north of the border call it, is definitely a Scots seabird, and a most delightful species to look at. It was at Fleswick Bay, however, that I was able to examine a freshly dead corpse which had been deposited by the ebbing tide – an unexpected opportunity to study the black bill with its bright orange gape, the red legs contrasting sharply with shiny black claws. The sleek deep brown plumage and the very obvious white wing-patch were the bird's summer plumage. In winter the black guillemot assumes a different appearance altogether, becoming white beneath, mottled above; at this stage it can look surprisingly grebe-like, though the white wing bar and auk-like bill still identify it. The puffin and the guillemot lay but one egg, but the black guillemot often produces two, laid without the benefit of nesting material in a hole or crevice sheltered from the elements. Here, after an incubation period of 26 days, the young hatch, and in a further 35 days they are fledged and independent.

The Chough

I am often accused by friends of having an ornithological love affair with St Bees, which I suppose is true, although to be honest I feel more like a spurned suitor. I return to the cliffs so often partly because I am confused by that delightful member of the Corvid family, the chough (*Pyrrhocorax pyrrhocorax*). Although choughs are still to be seen around these cliffs they no longer breed here; they may well have made the short sea journey (twenty miles) from the Isle of Man where they still breed in some numbers. The chough, like the rest of the crow family, is a real character and gives the impression of enjoying life to the full. The plumage glistens black and the red legs and downcurved bill complete the picture of elegance, while the lifestyle is tailormade for cliff dwelling. The nest is set in cracks and crevices away from the gusting winds which the adults easily master, being wonderfully co-ordinated aerobats. When many less efficient species head out to sea to avoid being driven into cliffs, and others skulk on ledges, feathers ruffled, the chough soars and dives, twists and turns, apparently for no apparent reason beyond sheer enjoyment of its mastery over the elements. Like many other well-adapted species the chough finds food by means of a bill ideally shaped for its special purpose, extracting ants from the soil and grass on the cliff tops. Why then should such a well-equipped bird be shrinking in both range and population? The answer is not too far to seek; the rising human population with more leisure and greater mobility takes more seaside holidays. This has put pressure on the chough which is easily disturbed during the time it is incubating its eggs.

Choughs (Harold Platt)

The cliff tops at St Bees suit choughs, since gorse is present in some quantity, and this usually means the presence of ants which help to spread the seeds of the plant. The cliff tops also have extensive carpets of thyme, yellow or biting stonecrop, small scabious, foxglove and harebell.

The Legless Lizard

Here too is found a most interesting animal, the slow-worm (*Anguis fragilis*). This is surely the most maligned of all our native animals. Some call it the blind-worm – yet it is neither a worm nor blind – nor, in warm weather, is it slow. I was once asked to identify 'a poisonous snake' which had just been killed: again, this poor creature is not poisonous nor even a snake. Actually it is a legless lizard, and a dissection of a dead specimen will reveal remnants of limbs beneath that hard muscular skin which when struck by the summer sun glistens like beaten metal. Basking in the morning sun is a favourite pastime of reptiles in general, but lizards seem to 'enjoy' the experience more than snakes: that is an anthropomorphic response, but as snakes have no eyelids they cannot blink in apparent contentment, as lizards do.

Both snakes and lizards are cold-blooded, which is why they like basking on exposed rocks early in the morning. A cold-blooded animal has a blood temperature approximately the same as that of its

Slow-worm and young (Douglas F. Lawson)

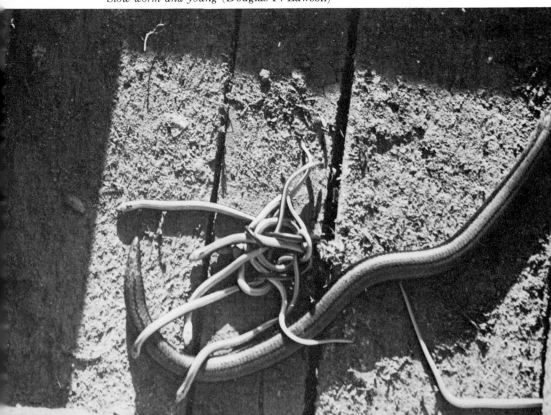

surroundings, which means that in cold weather it moves very slowly; once the day warms up it moves about faster than the so-called warm-blooded birds or mammals which are able to maintain a constant body temperature whatever the ambient conditions. At night, or in winter, animals such as the slow-worm do indeed become slow and eventually, must stop altogether. They face the opposite problem on long summer days; should the blood reach a temperature over 60° centigrade the enzymes which control the physiological processes would be destroyed. The animal senses the temperature increase and retires into a shady crevice. All this means that the best time to observe reptiles is early on a summer morning before the sun's heat has melted their sluggishness. For the photographer, a cold slow-worm is a much easier proposition than a warm one!

Slow-worms can live for a long time; several individuals have survived in captivity for over fifty years. Their diet consists of moving prey, with a marked preference for slugs and earthworms. Adult males, which fight fiercely in the breeding season, are larger than their mates and can measure up to 45cm (18in). The young are born in litters of about ten, but twenty have been recorded on occasions. They are sexually mature in their third or fourth year. It was at St Bees that I had the good fortune, one warm sunny morning to watch two mating slow-worms twined around each other, while a third chewed away at a writhing slug, which had itself been browsing on a clover leaf. Nothing gentle about the workings of nature – and there are few tougher habitats than a sea cliff in which to earn a living.

Granite Cliffs

There are fewer tougher cliffs than those of granite. In contrast to the sedimentary limestones, granite is of igneous origin, having been created deep within the bowels of the earth and then forced to the surface under intense pressures. Quartz, feldspar, hornblende and mica are all constituents of granite and ensure a strong resistance to erosion, but shortage of time is a phrase invented by modern man and unknown in nature. Though very slowly, the sea can eat away even at granite and produce huge and impressive caves and coves. Because of their complex make-up, granite cliffs vary in colour, with shades of pink, red, grey and blue that are a delight in any season. A visitor to the Scilly Isles, or Land's End or other areas of the Cornish coast, can but marvel at the colours and the rich cliff vegetation. Much of the coast of the Scillies is granite; the cliffs are not steep, apart from Penninnis and St Martin's Heads, but what they lack in height they more than make up for in colour. Ragwort, common birdsfoot and English stonecrop are all common and colourful.

19

Rhum and the Sea-Eagle

Granite is not confined to the south-west. Way up in the north-west the Inner Hebridean island of Rhum is composed of tough old granite, and in the north-east of Scotland the cliffs around Peterhead are flushed with the pink of feldspar. Rhum is of particular interest, since its 10,560 hectares (26,400 acres) have been owned by the Nature Conservancy since 1957. To the geologist the island is a fascinating spot. There is old sandstone to the north, but granite predominates towards the western end. The natural history of the island is rich. On the cliff ledges grow saw-wort, globe flower, angelica, eyebright, thyme, milkwort, thrift, English stonecrop, roseroot, golden rod and lovage. The birdlife on the cliffs is also interesting and here is a major breeding station of Manx shearwaters, which nest colonially in burrows in the loose gravelly soils high on the mountains. The biology of this incredible bird with the uncanny ability to find its breeding burrow in pitch darkness will be discussed at length in Chapter 8. Fulmars, kittiwakes and assorted auks populate the southern cliffs, and there are also breeding shags, Arctic tern and common tern, herring gull and lesser black-back gull. At the moment the blue-riband bird of the sea cliffs of Rhum is the white-tailed sea-eagle (*Haliaeetus albicilla*), formerly known as the erne. This was at one time a not uncommon resident species in Britain, but by 1916 it had been reduced to extinction, as much because of its tendency to come readily to carrion as to the development of accurate firearms. The old belief that the bird's yellow legs could be used to make a potion for curing jaundice cannot have helped. It is now only a vagrant to Britain, but – under the name of grey eagle – is distributed over both Europe and North America. Specimens recorded in Britain tend to be immatures wandering from Scandinavia. Adult birds are not migrants and therefore not likely to re-establish themselves on the breeding list. Since 1976 some 40 white-tailed sea-eagles have been introduced to Rhum, mainly from Norwegian stock. They have been immature birds but they have stayed put, and may well find the sea cliffs perfect for their eyries, in which the female will lay two unmarked eggs and then incubate them for about six weeks When the eaglets are hatched and growing rapidly both parents are needed to supply the ravenous young with small mammals, birds and fish. As with the similar-sized golden eagles (*Aquila chrysaetos*), which also breed on Rhum, the eggs are laid at two-day intervals so that one youngster is always older and stronger than the other. In times of plenty both young will be successfully reared, but should food become scarce then the stronger kills and consumes the weaker. In the world of nature any survival strategy that works tends to be retained.

Rhum has had a continuous record of human occupation since the Stone Age, from which time 'bloodstone' artefacts have been found.

The vegetation of the island has been gradually altered by man and his animals; primitive types of sheep and ponies can still be seen roaming the cliff ledges and mountainous slopes of Hallival and Trallval. As these names indicate, it was probably Scandinavian peoples who brought sheep and ponies to the island. Scotland's Highland clearances affected the islands too and by 1828 Rhum was evacuated, to be used only as a grazing area for the landowner's sheep. After a succession of deer-hunting, bird-shooting landlords, by 1902 Rhum was in the hands of Sir George Bullough of Accrington, who had built a huge castle at Kinloch, overlooking Loch Scresort. Sir George made his money from the manufacture of mill machinery at his works called Howard and Bullough. In 1957 Lady Monica Bullough sold the island to the Nature Conservancy Council and its wildlife has been carefully and expertly monitored ever since. Apart from the sea-eagle experiment, work is also being done on red deer, which can often be seen strolling along the edges of the cliffs superbly confident in their safety from the hunter's bullet and their own sure-footedness. They can also be confident of the stability of the granite under their feet, a feature not shared by some other cliff faces.

Sand and Clay Cliffs

Soft cliffs of sand and clay, often referred to as gault, are prominent around Folkestone. Here landslips, often of monumental proportions, are frequent – and similar instability occurs in Suffolk and around Cromer in Norfolk. The sandy rock, often interspersed with gravel, is easily undermined by the sea. Few plants and even fewer birds are able to make a permanent home in such unstable conditions, but those flowers which do manage to hang on include bird's-foot trefoil, harebell, kidney vetch and eyebright, the latter species growing among grasses.

Eyebright
This lovely little white-flowered annual (*Euphrasia officinalis*) is regarded as one of the thieves of the plant world. Beneath the ground it produces suckers which mingle with the roots of the grasses and probably extract some mineral or vitamin from them. Eyebright is in fact only a partial parasite and appears to do little, if any, harm to the grass. It has its own paired, bright green leaves up its stem, which terminates in an attractive cluster of small flowers, often white but sometimes a pale purple, the inside of the petals streaked with purple and spotted with yellow. The species shows great variation, which has led botanists to suggest a – varying – number of sub-species. The ancient herbalists recognised but one species, and thought it had an invaluable function in treating bad eyesight. They called it euphrasine.

The blind poet Milton wrote:

> To nobler sights
> Michael from Adam's eyes the film removed
> Which that false fruit which promised clearer sight
> Had bred; then purged with euphrasine and rue
> His visual orbs for he had much to see.

I wonder how long Milton persevered before realising that eyebright was not the answer to his problem. Culpeper, the Elizabethan herbalist, was also convinced of its value: 'If the herb was but as much used as it is neglected, it would half spoil the spectacle makers' trade . . . Tunned up with strong beer or mixed with sugar or a little mace or fennel seed, or eaten in broth . . . it will help and restore the sight decayed through age.' This belief originated in the old science of signatures; as the anonymous notes of another old apothecary point out, 'The purple and yellow spots and stripes which are upon the flowers of eyebright do very resemble the features of the eye as bloodshot etc. By which signature it hath been found that this herb is effectual for curing the same.'

The apothecary's shop was known as his 'office', the term we still use for a place of work, and a drug given the seal of approval was often named *officinalis* – a sort of hallmark or guarantee. The dandelion (*Taraxacum officinalis*), for treating the kidneys, and the eyebright were both approved drugs of the time, now of course superseded.

Basalt Cliffs

Sand and clay cliffs are problem areas for vegetation struggling for a firm anchorage, but the coastline's towering formations of basalt are solid enough. The rock contains augite and feldspar and is dark brown, fine-grained and crystalline. This is the rock which constitutes Staffa's Fingal's Cave and the even more impressive Giant's Causeway in Northern Ireland. Many of the Hebridean islands such as Skye, Mull, Muck, Eigg and Canna are of basalt; and birds frequenting their towering cliffs are safe from ground-dwelling predators. Sometimes we find isolated plugs of basalt, left as islands; once part of a complex of softer rocks they have been left to stand alone as their surroundings have been eroded away. The Bass Rock off North Berwick (see Chapter 8) is an example.

A little further to the south lie the basaltic Farne Islands, off the cliffs of Bamburgh, surmounted by a splendid castle.

Bamburgh and the Farnes are best visited in May, June and July when the bird breeding colonies are in full swing, or in autumn when the seals provide a fascinating courtship display. Beneath the castle the vegetation is amongst the most colourful in Britain, and on a hot day

Lady's bedstraw on Arbroath cliffs (Author)

the purple thyme and golden-red bird's-foot trefoil ooze perfume each
time they are pressed by a passing foot, the scent being wafted aloft by
the thermals of warm air rising from the ground. Silverweed, lady's (or
yellow) bedstraw, hop trefoil, tormentil, dog rose and sea storksbill are
all prominent below and upon the cliffs dominated by the castle walls.
Fulmars, on stiffened, almost arthritic-looking wings, herring gulls and
kittiwakes on bent ones, soar in and out of the crevices and off the
ledges. In good light every detail of the birds can be seen, including the
jet-black wing-tips of the kittiwakes. All our other gulls have the odd
patch of white to break up the uniformity of the dark wing-tips; these
patches are referred to by ornithologists as wing-mirrors.

Lady's Bedstraw, Heartsease and Haresfoot
One is torn between looking up at the birds and down at the beauty of
such plants as lady's bedstraw, heartsease and delicate haresfoot trefoil
or clover. Lady's bedstraw (*Galium verum*) is a relative of goosegrass
but has no prickles. The woody rootstock is slender, but the plant is
hardy, as a perennial must be. The flower-bearing stems vary

23

considerably in length but are always found in pairs, each pair set crosswise to those next above and below. The dark green leaves, whorled round the stem in groups of six to eight, contrast sharply with the delicate fresh yellow of the flowers which carry a faint but persistent scent. Each individual flower is tiny, but they are grouped in a thick panicle, giving the impression of greater size. Lady's bedstraw always grows in dry situations, and well-drained cliff tops and sand dunes are ideal for it.

In times gone by the plant was regarded as functional as well as decorative. Curtis, in his *Flora Londiniensis*, remarks that 'an ingenious gentleman conversant in dyeing assured me that it was a plant highly deserving of culture as an article in that business; for the roots though not so large as madder produced a brighter colour.' The colour referred to is red and not yellow, as an examination of the roots of lady's bedstraw would soon show. The generic name *Galium* is from the Greek word for milk, the plant possessing sufficient acidity to be used to curdle milk for butter- or cheese-making. Hence the old English name for bedstraw is cheese-rennet and the French call it *caille-lait*.

It had medical uses too. The flowers were boiled in olive oil and used to treat burns and scalds; it was also applied to the feet of tired travellers and rubbed upon aching joints and sinews; in the halcyon heyday of the country house, the footmen who accompanied the coaches of the rich made good use of it. A final useful attribute of lady's bedstraw is that it can coagulate blood and therefore act as an effective styptic.

In the Middle Ages it was known as 'stae Mariae stramen', Latin for Our Lady's bedstraw: the legend was that Our Lady not only found no room at the inn but was obliged to give birth on a bed of *Galium verum*, which was rewarded by having its flower colour changed from silver to gold.

The heartsease pansy's scientific name, *Viola tricolor*, refers to this delightful little flower's great variation of colours, based upon purple, yellow and white. The poet Cowley put it well.

> Gold, silver, purple are thy ornament,
> Thy rivals thou might scorn had'st thou but scent.

Heartsease (*Viola tricolor*) was often used by the old herbalists. Culpeper, the most famous of them, inclined to be over-critical of his rivals, mentions that 'This is the herb which such physicians as are licensed to blaspheme by authority, without danger of having their tongues burned through, called an Herb of the Trinity.' Heartsease is often said to have been used, as its name might imply, for the treatment of pains in the chest; it was certainly used against asthma and pleurisy, and also epilepsy and other diseases, though there is no evidence that it would be effective. Shakespeare seemed to know of other uses too. In *A Midsummer Night's Dream*, Oberon asserts:

> The juice of it on sleeping eyelids laid,
> Will make or man or woman madly dote
> Upon the next live creature that it sees.

Herrick also refers to the flower's use as a love-charm for 'retired Frolick ladies': he asks

> Love in pity of their tears
> And their loss in blooming years
> For their restless here-spent years
> Give them heart's ease turned to flowers.

In John Bunyan's *Pilgrim's Progress* a young man in the Valley of Humiliation is heard singing 'He that is down need fear no fall, he that is low no pride.' The guide says: 'I will dare to say this lad leads a merrier life and wears more of that herb called heartsease in his bosom than he that is clad in silk and velvet.'

So much then for the folklore of this little pansy. Looking at its botanical features, it has much more deeply cut foliage and larger stipules at the base of the leaves than other members of the violet family, and its stem is more branched. At the back of the flower is a spur, an elongation of the base of the lowest petal that is a characteristic feature of the violets. The flower is eventually succeeded by seed capsules; when they split the seeds are released into the wind and on the ground and thus distributed.

Haresfoot clover or haresfoot trefoil (*Trifolium arvense*) is sometimes less obvious than other plants around it, but take the time to sit amongst it; watch its furry blossoms bobbing at the slightest whisper of a summer breeze. It flowers from June to September in Britain, its range extending throughout Europe and well into western Asia. The hairy stems are slender but branch freely and carry the flowers in an upright posture. As you would expect in a trefoil, the leaves have three leaflets, in this case narrow and equal in size. The small white pea-like flowers are insignificant in themselves, but are massed in cylindrical terminal heads, usually fleshy-grey and very hairy. It is these furry structures that give the plant its name, which is of great antiquity. Early herbalists such as Gerard and Parkinson called it Lagopus (Greek *lagos*, a hare and *pus*, foot). In German it was *hasenfuss* and in French *pied du lievre*.

Puffins – and Eels

Photographing flowers is trying on the eyes and limbs, and I was stretching and having a good blink on the cliffs of Bamburgh when my attention was drawn to a line of birds flying inland from the sea, which

Puffin – the sea parrot (Brian W. Burnett)

was flowing in and already far up the beach. Even from a distance the
'jizz' of these birds identified them as members of the auk family – short
wings, dumpy bodies, small size, fast wing-beat. But which auk? My
binoculars soon picked up the multicoloured bill of a puffin. Just above
my head, the leader of a group of a dozen or so birds seemed to realise
that the flight path was wrong, banked sharply and headed off in the
direction of the Inner Farne. As it turned, a long, thin, silvery object fell
from its bill and spiralled its way earthwards, landing with a smack less
than 5m (16ft) from my feet. Not manna from heaven, but a biological
treasure in the form of a sand eel, the principal food of the puffin. It was
dead, but had been a magnificent specimen.

Sand eels are in fact elongated fish, not eels, and belong to the perch
order. Around the coasts of Britain there are five species, all important
to many of the creatures of and around our coastal waters. In the sub-
order *Ammodytoidei*, they are: the common sand eel (*Ammodytes
marinus*), the greater sand eel (*Hyperoplus (Ammodytes) lanceolatus*),
the smooth sand eel (*Gymnammodytes semisquamatous*), the lesser sand
eel (*Ammodytes tobianus*) and *Hyperoplus (Ammodytes) immaculatus*,
which has no English name. Sand eels are an essential link in the marine
food chain. The common sand eel can live for up to nine years, often

shoaling in enormous numbers, preferring seas of a depth of 20–40m (65–131ft) with sandy bottoms. It is one of the few marine fish that deposit their spawn on the seabed. Its breeding period lasts from December to February. After hatching the larvae become part of the plankton, at first being purely vegetarian but later eating invertebrates and their larvae. A feeding pattern has been detected, as a result of intensive research which was undertaken because they are used in the manufacture of fish meal. They seem to feed at dawn and dusk, and spend the rest of the time either buried in the sand, or idling about close to the surface, being hunted by seabirds and predatory fish. A length of 25cm (10in) is rarely exceeded and the weight is up to about 32g (just over 1oz). The one which my friend the puffin approaching Bamburgh Castle dropped at my feet was 15cm long (6in) and weighed 18g (just over $\frac{1}{2}$oz).

I followed the puffins' line of flight towards Staple Island, an east-coast Mecca for birds and birdwatchers alike, having one of the finest seabird breeding colonies in Europe. I well remember a trip I made to the island in 1979, in a small boat bobbing gently on a blue sea under a sweltering sun, one of the few such precious days in a notoriously poor summer. There were kittiwakes, puffins, razorbills, eiders, lesser black-backed gulls, herring gulls, ringed plover, oyster-catchers and on occasions Arctic terns, though these are usually restricted to the Inner Farne. The dominant flower without any doubt is the sea campion (*Silene maritima*). To the south of the island are the isolated rock stacks known locally as the Pinnacles. These are literally smothered in the dominant bird of Staple Island, the guillemot.

Shags and Guillemots
Concentrating first, however, upon the shag my attention was immediately focused upon a battle-royal taking place between a shag and a kittiwake; the latter I had always considered to be the least aggressive species of the gull tribe, and indeed this kittiwake was sitting upon its nest, minding its own business and brooding two youngsters. But from its otherwise neatly fashioned nest a few pieces of seaweed were protruding, and the shag, whose own nest was further along the ledge, had looked upon this with a covetous eye, sidled slowly and slyly sideways, finally making a sudden determined snatch at the weed. The kittiwake flushed in alarm and the youngsters peeped their fright as the shag tugged – but the seaweed stuck fast. The shag looked puzzled, pulled again, stood back a little, almost toppling off the narrow ledge – and shook its head. The parent kittiwake had now decided to take a hand and flew headlong at the shag, which retaliated by stabbing angrily at its assailant with its bill and then returned to the task of pinching the weed. Eighteen times the kittiwake attacked and

Shags with young on the Farne Islands (Author)

seventeen times the shag repelled it. After the eighteenth assault the shag gave up the struggle and shambled away along the ledge to where its mate was brooding three reptilian-looking babies. She turned her head away from him as if to say 'You lost – again!'

The trespassing shag, I noticed, was ringed, as were many birds here, and a number had a second coloured ring as well, thus allowing very accurate field identification.

The shag (*Phalocrocorax aristotelis*) has been used as a sort of indicator species to detect the presence of poisons in our seas. In the magazine *British Birds* (Vol 71, 1978) a paper 'Further Seabird Deaths from Paralytic Shellfish Poisoning' by Armstrong, Hudson, Coulson and Hawkey, reported that in 1968 many seabirds perished as a result of what has become known as PSP. Many shellfish are filter feeders and as they strain their food from the water they pick up a protozoan animal, *Gonyaulax tamarensis*. The population of this organism can reach monumental proportions and because of its colour it has caused a 'red tide' every year since 1968. *Gonyaulax* produces a poison which affects the nervous system; eventually this poison works its way through the food chain, and for some reason the shag appears to be the most sensitive seabird. The four workers discovered that 63 per cent of the birds breeding on the Farnes died as a result of PSP in 1975, when *Gonyaulax* was particularly prolific.

Obviously much more work on the problem is needed, for although the shag population has so far recovered quickly this cannot be guaranteed in future years. I was once asked at the end of a lecture, 'Why should we bother about the deaths of a few insignificant birds?' The answer to that naive question is a serious one. Leaving aside the wish that most of us have to take care of our wild creatures, we must not forget that the shag is at the top of the marine food chain; with our taste for fish and other sea-foods we ourselves occupy a similar position. Deaths from PSP, whatever the organism involved, must be most carefully monitored.

The shag has earned many vernacular names, including 'Isle of Wight parson' – from a distance it does look clerical. In Ireland it is called the 'green cormorant', as it takes on a distinctly green hue when the sunlight reflects from its oily plumage. Up in the Orkney Islands it goes by the name of 'green scout', no doubt from its habit of standing on outlying rocks looking out to sea. Another of its local names I found puzzling until I developed my pictures from Staple Island: in parts of northern England the shag is called the cotton-heap – and the young shags in the photographs looked just like heaps of dark brown cottonwool.

Though often confused with its close relative the cormorant, the shag has several distinguishing points – one being that it lacks the cormorant's large white patch under the throat. The shag also has a pronounced crest, and a yellow inside to its bill. It is more restricted in range than the cormorant, being almost exclusively confined to the coast. Cormorants are frequently recorded at inland sites – although careful censusing techniques have shown, surprisingly to me at least, that the shag has a breeding population of over 31,000 pairs, whereas the cormorant has only 8,000 breeding pairs. The number of eggs laid by the shag is said to vary between two and six; they are incubated by both birds for thirty-three days before the cotton-heaps chip their way out. The nest is constructed almost entirely of seaweed and at the end of the

29

Guillemots (Brian W. Burnett)

fledgling period, fifty days or so after hatching, the stench can be overpowering, especially in hot weather. The young are of course fed on regurgitated fish, which contributes strongly to the malodorous atmosphere. Shags sometimes breed at the age of three, but more often start during their fourth year.

The guillemot (*Uria aalge*) has been estimated to be Britain's most numerous breeding seabird. The Seabird Group (see Cramp, Bourne and Saunders in Bibliography) estimated that in 1969 there were 577,000 pairs. It is another member of the auk family, and looks very similar to a small penguin, although auks have not yet lost the power of flight. Guillemots are excellent swimmers and spend much of the time on or just under the water – occupying much the same niche in the northern hemisphere as penguins take in the southern. So they are particularly vulnerable to oil pollution of the sea (see Chapter 9).

They breed in huge colonies on ledges, sometimes on very steep cliffs, and on offshore islands. Staple Island and its pinnacles are excellent sites for them. The female lays only one egg, but it is huge compared to her body size – and is pear-shaped, a feature that probably has some survival value: if it is left unattended in a strong wind, it will rotate on its own axis rather than roll off the ledge; it simply spins like a top. Some ornithologists doubt this theory, but no other explanation of the egg's unusual shape has been found.

Guillemot eggs are a buff colour, spotted or heavily blotched with various shades of brown, though they vary and a bluish egg without markings may appear. Both sexes incubate, and in a peculiar manner: the egg is held on top of the webbed feet and loose skin from the bird's rear is stretched over egg and feet by a skilful manipulation with the bill. The incubation period lasts about thirty-two days.

Once the young have hatched, the obvious danger is that they may get pushed to their deaths. At this stage, however, the adult birds are in fairly tolerant mood, and any displaced chick will be brooded by an adult, an invaluable survival pattern for a bird breeding in huge colonies in exposed and precipitous places. It seems that after the fierce sorting-out of territories before breeding, and the acquisition of space for egg-laying, much of the aggression subsides.

The young birds are still small and unable to fly when the adults persuade them to jump from the nest site on to the water. Both parents contrive to feed the chick until it learns to dive and capture small invertebrates and fish for itself.

An adult guillemot measures some 40cm (16in) long and from a distance the plumage looks distinctly black and white, but the closer the bird is approached the browner it appears. This is in contrast to the darker and shinier razorbill, which also has a much thicker bill than the guillemot. Some guillemots have a white ring round the eye, from there leading towards the neck. The distribution of these 'bridled' birds has been the subject of long and intensive studies. At one stage it was thought that the bridled form was a separate species: Professor Macgillivray in his *Manual of British Birds Complete*, published in the 1840s, names it *Uria troile*, the foolish guillemot. But it is now known that the marking is due to a recessive genetic character. An enquiry into the incidence of bridling was initiated by the British Trust for Ornithology in 1938 and has continued at intervals ever since. Apparently the frequency of the bridled form increases as you move from south to north. In southern England only 1 per cent of the guillemots are bridled; in the Shetlands 26 per cent, in the Faroes 34 per cent and in Iceland 60 per cent. The figure normally accepted for the Farnes is about 4 per cent, and on Staple Island I decided to do a random count of about 400 birds to see if this figure was borne out. My count was nowhere near large enough to be statistically significant, but of my 384 guillemots, 16 were bridled, exactly 4 per cent – pure luck, but it does endorse the accepted figures. On the island of Canna in the Outer Hebrides I counted another 400 guillemots, of which 41 were bridled, just over 10 per cent.

Guillemots moult in July, and from then on, often until well into

November, the dorsal surface is a greyish-brown and the throat and cheeks become white, apart from a small black line extending back from the eye. Most of the winter is spent at sea, but during this time the birds may pay periodic visits to the breeding sites, apparently checking that everything at home is as they left it. I have noticed that many colonial birds do this, but guillemots are probably more noticeable because of the large numbers involved.

The Seals

It is not only the birdlife of the Farnes that makes them memorable; the seals are well worth a visit in their own right. Britain has two breeding seals, the common seal (*Phoca vitulina*) and the grey seal (*Halichoerus grypus*); it is the latter that has caused such a maelstrom in the political waters lapping the Farnes. Our coasts are also visited on occasions by five other species, the ringed seal (*Phoca hispida*), the harp seal (*Phoca groen landica*), the bearded seal (*Erignathus barbatus*), the hooded seal (*Crystophora cristata*) and the walrus (*Odobenus rosmarus*), which made the headlines in September 1981.

The distinction between the two 'British' species is a relatively easy one. The grey seal is considerably larger and can reach a length of over 2.5m (7ft), compared to the 1.75m (5ft) of the common seal. The whole body is not often seen in a casual glance at a seal in the water; usually only the head appears, but that is enough to identify the species. The common seal has a small head, and the bridge between its nose and forehead gives a 'doggy' profile, complete with muzzle. The nostrils touch at their lowest point, forming a V. The grey seal, on the other hand, has a large flat head with no muzzle, and the nostrils are separate and parallel.

The distribution of the grey seal is unique in the annals of seal natural history (see Hewer, Bibliography). There seem to be three distinct populations, centred on the Baltic, the western Atlantic and our own eastern-Atlantic group. There is evidence that the eastern-Atlantic population should be regarded as a sub-species; the British greys, for example, breed in autumn rather than spring, and favour solid ground rather than icefloes for dropping their pups. Both these characteristics differ from those of the Baltic and western-Atlantic groups. The distribution of the grey seal has not yet been thoroughly investigated, and our knowledge of its biology is even more deficient, although some progress has been made in recent years. It is accepted that the mammalian way of life evolved on land, and the respiratory system, consisting of lungs and associated vascular and musculature systems, is designed for land animals. Seals have had to evolve answers to all the problems man himself faces when trying to penetrate the depths of the seas: the need for an oxygen supply, the difficulties caused by cold and

Grey seal cow (Bill Paton/Nature Photographers Ltd)

the tremendous unrelenting pressure in deep, dark waters. Some of the solutions have proved surprising to say the least.

The lungs do not seem to be particularly large and in any case seals exhale before diving! The thorax cavity, however, is so constructed that it is flattened by high pressure rather than injured by it. If there is no oxygen available in the lungs then there is little point in wasting blood going to collect it, and so seals enter into a physiological state known as bradycardia. The heartbeat is drastically slowed, its strength reduced to an absolute minimum, just sufficient for the blood to be pushed along the carotid artery and to keep the brain supplied with oxygen. A huge circular muscle (called the sphincter muscle) contracts and shuts off the huge veins leading to the heart.

The problem that then remains is for the seal to find an alternative supply of oxygen while it is under water. It was assumed at one time that having a high red blood-cell count might be the answer, but research has shown that the seal's is not significantly higher than our own, and much less than that of some people living at high altitudes.

The solution actually seems to be twofold. Seal muscle has large quantities of a substance called myoglobin, which can carry even more oxygen attached to its molecule than can our own red pigment, haemoglobin. Thus while the seal is on the surface and breathing normally, these 'reserve tanks' of myoglobin are recharged, to be drawn upon when the animal is submerged. The second adaptation of seals is that they can run into what has been called 'oxygen debt'. During normal respiration, carbohydrate is burned in oxygen to release energy but, in times of oxygen shortage, say when the seal is under pressure from predators and must stay submerged, the protein of muscle tissue can be broken down to release energy and in doing so requires a lot less oxygen. This 'oxygen-debt' is repaid when the seal has eaten and has the leisure to lie on the surface of the sea, rebuild its protein reserves and draw air into its landlubber's lungs.

Grey seals take an extensive list of food items. Squids are a favourite, but many large fish, some of commercial interest, are caught, along with a few seabirds unwise enough to roost too close to a hunting animal. Two black-headed gulls close to Staple Island once showed me how rash they can be. A seal had caught a large fish and was ripping it to pieces, tossing it about as a cat throws a mouse. Suddenly these two gulls dived down at the seal; it automatically submerged and the birds squabbled over the scraps of fish floating on the surface. The seal came up and looked quizzically at the gulls, the rest of his fish still gripped in his jaws. The gulls attacked again, and once more the seal dived; once more the intrepid pair gathered the scraps. The seal appeared yet again, then gulped down the fish and was gone.

The seal's preference for fish makes it unpopular with fishermen, especially those pursuing our dwindling stocks of salmon (see Chapter 2). It is probably no exaggeration to say that one of the greatest controversies in British natural history circles at the moment concerns the grey seal – to cull or not to cull. Too many naturalists seem to sit on the fence. In my view the seals should be left alone. When the first human settlers moved into the areas exposed by the melting ice some 12,000 years ago, they found the grey seal waiting; they chased it, hacked it to pieces, ate its flesh, wore its skin, burned its oil. Gradually the seals became warier and moved out to offshore islands. Fishermen followed them, driven on by the need to earn money.

By 1914, the plight of these delightful sea creatures was so desperate that the Grey Seal Protection Act was passed, though it was hoped to repeal it after five years once the depleted population had recovered. All the Act did was to protect the grey seal for its reproductive period, which lasts from about 1 October to 15 December. As usual the Act was ignored by those who risk any fine provided the potential profits are large enough. It could not therefore be repealed and in 1932 it was

Killer whale

necessary to extend the close season at both ends, to operate from 1 September to 31 December. The Act itself, however, had no real teeth; it was as dead as those little seal pups hammered to death with clubs. In 1970 came the Conservation of Seals Act, largely a result of the efforts of the President of the Mammal Society, Lord Cranbrook. It was touch and go, however, great resistance being generated in the House of Lords, where some sleepy members still seemed under the impression that the wicked seals were snatching lifegiving fish out of children's mouths. They did not, and indeed do not, care to reflect that we have chased the seals away from our extensive coastline, and now wish to chase them even further. This is not a common animal that is at risk: the grey seal is now the rarest of the seals. It must be preserved, even at the expense of a few – a very few – fish.

What Eats the Grey Seal?
What could possibly swallow a 210cm (7ft), 300kg (660lb) grey seal in its entirety? What could reduce a herd of these predators of our seas to a state of mad hysteria? The answer is the grampus, otherwise known as the killer whale (*Orcinus orca*). I certainly did not expect to see these splendid beasts so close inshore, but an extract from field notes written while seawatching from a boat just off Staple Island shows just how suddenly nature can throw up unexpected excitement.

> Four killer whales seen 20m from bow – one about 9m long, no beak noted, but snout round; prominent dorsal fin slightly recurved. Female? Another animal with tall triangular fin. Male? Female dived 32 times in 17 minutes, no dive lasting longer than 12 seconds and averaging 7.31 seconds. Group never more than 100m from boat and circling. Male much less active diving 9 times averaging 8.64 seconds. Distinctive black and white pattern clearly observed in all four animals. Also noted a white patch behind the eye and an area of grey just behind the dorsal fin.

Very little is known of the natural history of this species of whale, or indeed of many others, and dead specimens are urgently required for examination by experts: the University of Cambridge are always anxious to hear of any animal washed up and will make a journey to visit their 'prize'. Contact the Dolphin Survey Project, Department of Anatomy, University of Cambridge, Downing Street, Cambridge, CB2 3DY. Tel (0223) 68665. Although we need to know much more about the killer whale, we do have some information available. It is a pleasure to report, for once, that the killer whale is not yet uncommon. It is however declining in some parts of its range which can truly be considered to be worldwide, nearing both poles depending upon the season. Males can reach 10m in length and in contrast to what was formerly believed the females are not a great deal shorter. They swim fast – some rate them as the quickest in the seas – and are the aquatic equivalent to a pack of hunting dogs. Fearless and relentless in search of prey, they range the seas, and will tear apart animals much larger than themselves. To them a seal is a between-meals snack, although they do take fish and squid; they have been known to attack a whale carcase being towed behind a factory ship.

Basalt cliffs are indeed impressive habitats, as this account of their wildlife has shown. I may have given the impression that cliff types fit neatly into a prearranged system. The natural world, however, is never like this and thrives on chaos. Some sea cliffs may be a complex mixture of the types referred to above, and may also contain slate, shale or even millstone grit. This should not worry the naturalist since such a complex system will be richer in flora and the fauna which often depend upon it. It must also be true to say that each area is unique, since it will be subjected to differing tidal and atmospheric conditions, receive more or less spray – or human interference. This also applies to the habitats discussed in the next chapter, our estuaries and their associated mudflats.

2
Estuaries and Mudflats

Although no two estuaries can ever be identical, they will have certain features in common. A river rising in the hills first hurries down its steep-sided valley and gradually slows down to a meander when many of its suspended solids fall out of the slackening current to form mud banks. With a speed depending upon the physical geography of the river itself, and the rainfall, the water will eventually reach the sea's variable ebb and flow. When the freshwater river current meets the saline flood tide, the two will cancel each other out, and rich suspensions of solids will be deposited from both sources: this area is the estuary.

Britain is well endowed with estuaries (or, in Scotland, firths) but many are under threat from industrial enterprises. Seabird deaths on the polluted Mersey estuary, for example, have been much in the news in recent years; many oil terminals are already established and more planned, along the edges of estuaries. Here we look at life-forms found in estuaries with low pollution levels, those full of interest for the naturalist, but Chapter 9 considers the problems of pollution.

In estuaries untroubled by human interference, the main adaptation needed by animals and plants is a way of dealing with the very variable salinity of estuarine waters. The salt of the sea originates from erosion of the land; rivers pour their very slightly salty water into the sea, and as the amount of water is kept approximately constant by evaporation, the percentage of dissolved solid matter in sea water is high, in the order of 3.5 per cent, and gradually rising. Common salt (sodium chloride) is the main solid constituent.

Composition of Sea water	Percentage
Water	96.4
Common salt	2.8
Magnesium chloride	0.4
Magnesium sulphate	0.2
Calcium sulphate	0.1
Potassium chloride	0.1
	100.0

The mudflats on the National Nature Reserve at Leigh Marshes, Essex, showing the early stages of saltmarsh development (see Chapter 3) (P. Wakely/Nature Conservancy Council)

Most animals, including humans, have some salt in their tissues and without it would die; retaining enough of it, especially in hot climates where salt is lost as sweat, is quite a problem. Roman soldiers on duty in such areas were often paid in salt or given extra 'salt money' to purchase it: this is the origin of the word salary (Latin *salarium*). Life is believed to have begun in the sea, which explains why so many body fluids contain salt; the saltiness of sea water presents few problems to those animals which evolved there. In time a great many life-forms evolved strategies to live in fresh water. To well-adapted fresh-water animals, life in saline water would not be possible; and likewise many sea-dwelling organisms cannot survive being immersed in fresh water.

What then happens in an estuary, where the sea water mixes with the river outflow, and living organisms find themselves in a sort of

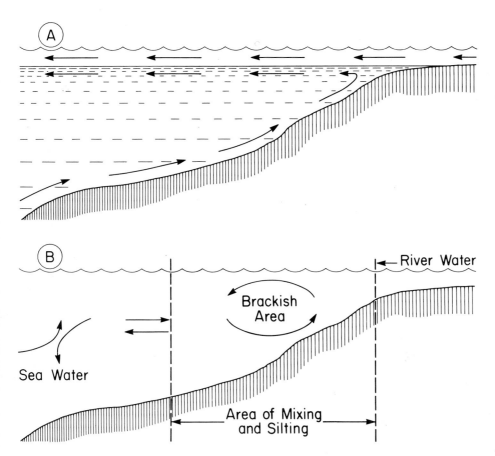

The formation of estuarine deposits: seawater is denser than fresh water, so the river water tends to float on top of the brine (A); the tides stir these two waters together and allow silt from the river to be deposited (B)

biological limbo? Fresh water is lighter than sea water and tends to flow outwards, sliding over the top of the denser brine. However there will be an area of mixing, which is termed brackish water, and it is here that the genius of evolutionary strategies will be tested to the full.

Three invertebrate animals which can regulate their body fluids in response to sudden variations in salinity are the shore crab, the estuarine prawn and the shrimp. Among the vertebrates, fish are usually defined as either fresh-water or marine, but three species in particular have learned to cope with the considerable problems involved: the three-spined stickleback, the salmon and the eel. Thus we have six organisms which have succeeded in developing different strategies that all obviously work.

The Shore Crab (Carcinus maenas)

This is certainly the most abundant and sometimes the only species of crab found in our estuaries. It survives there because it is able to maintain its body fluids at a higher concentration than the water around it; this condition is termed hyperosmotic. Osmosis is one of the fundamental laws of physical science: where a semi-permeable membrane separates a concentrated solution from a weaker solution, the weaker solution will pass through the membrane to the stronger solution. A living membrane is semi-permeable, and if the crab's blood is of higher concentration than the sea water, then water will enter its body. This does not matter provided the animal has an efficient method of getting rid of excess fluid – it must produce a high volume of urine. The crab even has a safety device to meet the reverse situation. From time to time crabs may get stranded in a brackish pool, where a combination of neap tides, hot weather and low rainfall has increased the concentration of salt so much that it exceeds that of the crab's blood. The pool water would then tend to draw water from the crab and dehydrate it. But the crab's blood salts can increase until they are as dense as those of the water in the pool, thus maintaining the status quo until the time of rain or full tide.

The complex chemistry involved here has been acquired by only a few species. Shore crabs have 'learned' to live in estuary conditions and actually breed there; the only recurring problem that they cannot live with is the low winter temperatures encountered in shallow waters. They respond to these by migrating into the deeper waters of the sea, which always remain above freezing point. Marking experiments on shore crabs during the summer show that they have no territorial boundaries but prefer wandering at random in search of food, which consists of living animal material or carrion.

Crabs belong to the order of invertebrate, jointed-limbed animals called arthropods, which in turn are classified into insects (3 pairs of legs), spiders (4 pairs of legs), crustaceans (5–10 pairs) and myriapods (which all have more than 10 pairs of legs). Together with lobsters, prawns and shrimps, crabs are crustaceans, in a group called decapods (*deca*, ten, *pod*, foot): they have 1 pair of pincers called chelipeds and 4 pairs of walking legs. True crabs, including the shore crab, have a small flap-like abdomen which is folded neatly beneath the body. The sex can be determined by looking at the shape of this flap – females have a broad flap with 7 segments, whereas on the smaller males it is narrower, with 5 segments. An interesting reaction can be observed if a crab is carefully picked up and gently dropped on to its back (the shell is called the carapace). The female immediately folds her walking legs across her abdomen, covering her abdominal flap. Males do not react in this way so it seems that this behaviour is the female's built-in reflex to protect her eggs, which she carries beneath her abdominal flap.

The shore crab's colour varies from browny-orange to green. In laboratory-based experiments, if a group of crabs is divided into two equal 'teams', one group being placed in a tank with a white background, the others in a darker tank, it is found that an appreciable number, though not all, are able to change colour, chameleon-like, to match their background. This is an admirable protective strategy for the species, but it should serve as a warning to any naturalist trying to identify *Carcinus maenas* by colour. The only sure way to identify the species is by finding the five unique sharp toothlike structures on the edge of the carapace on either side of the eyes.

All species, including humans, have biological rhythms, bringing periods when their activities are at their most efficient. Shore crabs seem to be most active at high spring tides, especially when they occur at night; again, laboratory experiments have shown that crabs dislike bright light. One ingenious scheme involves putting a crab in a box with sufficient seaweed and brine to keep it happy. The box is then placed on a see-saw arrangement which will tilt each time the crab moves. A pointer is attached to the box and the apparatus connected to a recording drum. Even when removed from the sea and kept in the dark, the crab still becomes most active at the time of the high tide. Like many other – probably all other – living organisms, it has its own built-in biological clock.

The main breeding activity also takes place at night, and great fun can be had by walking your local estuary armed with a torch, crab-watching. (Once again let me stress the value of a set of local tide tables, which should be referred to before setting out and wrist watches should also be checked.) Crab copulation often takes place when the female is moulting, after which she is said to be 'in berry'. At this time she tends to prefer shallow water, and so the winter estuary will have larger numbers of pregnant females than either males or non-pregnant females. The eggs can be seen as separate objects, and cannot therefore be mistaken for the eggs of a very common parasite of the crab, a creature called the sea-barnacle (*Sacculina carcini*), whose eggs are enclosed in a single yellow sac stuck to the host's abdomen. The larva or zoeae which hatches from a crab's egg takes its place in the floating plankton of the sea which is so important in the diet of many fish. It is easily recognised (although you do need a low-powered microscope) by a long spine-like structure on the head, with another at the opposite end of the body, pointing backwards. After several moults the larva changes into the megalopa stage, and settles on the bottom of the shallow sea, where it changes into a young crab, and the metamorphosis is complete.

Shore crabs live for three or four years and may reach a size of 10cm (4in) across the carapace, although the larger specimens tend to be

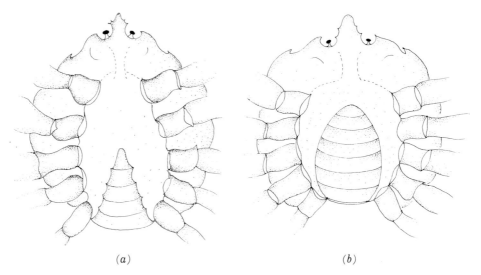

(a)   (b)

Abdominal flaps of (a) male and (b) female shore crab

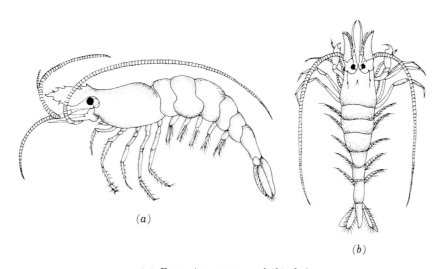

(a)

(b)

(a) Estuarine prawn and (b) shrimp

found in deeper water and a 'good estuary crab' will be in the order of 5–7.5cm (2–3in). Their hard outer skeleton must be shed before they can grow, and the crab wriggles out backwards through a slit which develops along the rear edge. Until the new carapace is hard, the moult (or ecdysis) is not complete, and the soft crab is particularly vulnerable to predators, foremost of these being the hordes of gulls that frequent estuaries. Escaping their attentions is difficult enough for a crab at any time, but it does at least have the strange ability to regenerate any limb lost in a brush with a predator, or a rival during courtship, or as the result of an accident. That life is tough for the shore crab may be judged from the fact that nearly one-fifth of the population show evidence of having had to regrow at least one limb.

Estuary Prawns and Shrimps
The genus *Palaemonetes* includes about twenty species, most of which are restricted to fresh water, though three are totally marine. Five species are found in the hybrid world of brackish waters, and of these the estuarine prawn *Palaemonetes varians* is by far the commonest. Much research has been done to discover how this prawn keeps the concentration of salts in its blood in balance with the ever-changing estuary waters. When it finds itself in the open sea it keeps its blood concentration below that of the water; this means that water is withdrawn from its body fluids by means of osmosis, and the prawn compensates for this by drinking large quantities of sea water. When the estuarine water salts are 60–70 per cent of the concentration of normal sea water, they are at the same level as the prawn's blood; the two fluids are in balance. As the river pours into the estuary and the concentration of the water is diluted, the prawn maintains the concentration of its blood, and thus water enters its body from the environment. It compensates for this by producing large quantities of urine.

Gurney (in 1924) studied the development of the larvae, a formidable achievement since they normally have six stages; and at each moult the number of appendages increases. Some of the younger types swim on their backs, but as they reach the adult stage they begin to swim the right way up. Once the adult form is reached, a further fifteen moults may be necessary before the prawn is sexually mature. Considering its size, it has a formidable pair of pincers; it preys on worms, which abound both in sand and in estuary mud (see Chapter 6), a diet it shares with the shrimp.

Shrimps are a well-known table delicacy, but the attractive pink colour seen on the plate differs greatly from the greeny-grey, speckled with light brown, of the living animal, *Crangon vulgaris*. Shrimps and prawns are often confused, even the fishmonger referring to 'pink prawns' as shrimps. The main difference between shrimps and prawns is that the part of the carapace which projects between the eyes is very short in the shrimp, but in the prawn it forms a long toothed beak-like structure. Shrimps also have a much more flattened body than prawns.

They are nocturnal in habit, crawling over the sand or mud using their last two pairs of legs, and they can also swim, but neither method of locomotion is as efficient as in the prawn. The shrimp, however, does cope well with fluctuating salinity, keeping the blood's salt concentration steady, constantly monitoring changes and regulating accordingly. In winter, shrimps move down the estuaries and out to sea. As with crabs, the females seem better able to cope with extreme conditions than their mates, and they are the last to leave in winter and the first to return in spring. The females also live four or five years, to the males' three. Their breeding efficiency seems to suffer if they choose to carry their berries around an estuary instead of taking them on a sea journey: one brood is usual in an estuary but two are produced in the sea.

Shrimps are caught commercially on the Dee, on the coasts of Kent and Essex and especially in Morecambe Bay. From Flookborough near Grange-over-Sands the method is mechanised, and tractors chasing out into an ebbing tide are an everyday sight; in contrast, the shrimp-catchers of Stolford in Bridgwater Bay fish on a flood tide, using staked nets, a method which has been in operation for centuries and was even recorded in the Domesday Book. Shrimps can be caught in small numbers by fishing in rock-pools or raking the damp sand into which they burrow, being content to await the return of the tide before going hunting. Many are captured at this time by the probing bills of the ringed plover or the sanderling; but who would expect a shrimp in a rock-pool to be tackled by the 'tiddler' of the inland pond – the three-spined stickleback?

The Sticklebacks

Although this stickleback (*Gasterosteus aculeatus*) is commoner in fresh water, it regularly migrates into estuaries and lives quite happily there. Indeed in the northern seas of Britain it even thrives several miles offshore, although how it regulates its salt levels is not well understood. An interesting recent discovery, however, is that the number of bony plates along the side of the body varies as salinity and latitude increase. Fresh-water specimens in Belgium were found to have only four or five plates, whereas those living in brackish waters can have between twenty and thirty. It will be interesting to see what part, if any, these plates play in controlling salt levels.

The three-spined stickleback, 7.5cm (3in) long, is a well-documented species and the male's behaviour in constructing a nest in which he induces gravid females to deposit their eggs is fully described in many natural history books. In the breeding period his breast and belly are glowing red. The stickleback family in general is typified by having isolated dorsal spines (they are not fins) which can be erected and also have a locking device, which gives considerable protection against predators. The ten-spined stickleback (*Pungitus pungitus*) is confined to fresh water. At 5cm (2in), our smallest fresh-water fish is the three-spined stickleback, one that as we have seen can cope with both fresh and brackish waters. The fifteen-spined stickleback (*Spinachia spinachia*) is larger, reaching 20cm (8in) and is a marine fish, found in harbours and rock-pools during the summer. Although this is a solitary species and therefore not easily found, it does seem to be associated with eel grass – an imported plant which, as we shall see in Chapter 3, is also a favourite of the Brent goose.

The fifteen-spined stickleback's breeding season is from April to early July, during which time the nest-building male takes on handsome breeding colours, in this species various shades of blue, designed to persuade as many females as possible to leave their precious eggs in his care. The nest is a scrape, usually among fronds of seaweed, and he is just as faithful in protecting the young as the three-spined. There is a suggestion that the exertions of breeding cause the death of the adults, but this is not yet proved.

The Eel

The fifteen-spined stickleback may be regarded as a permanent resident of our estuaries, whereas the eel and the salmon are more like passage migrants. The eel is on its way from fresh water to breed at sea (behaviour known as catadromous); the salmon feeds at sea but returns to its native river to breed (anadromous behaviour).

When living in fresh water our eels (*Anguilla anguilla*) are generally known as 'yellow eels', due to the colour of the belly. The males, smaller than their mates, can measure up to 40cm (16in) and may have spent as long as twelve years in fresh water before feeling the breeding urge that impels them to return to the sea. The females may wait as long as nineteen years, and by this time may be 60cm (2ft) long.

The hormones which initiate the journey also cause a change in body colour, and those on migration are called 'silver eels'. All their time and energy are now devoted to reaching the breeding grounds across hundreds of miles of ocean. Even the gut is digested and finally disappears, so that feeding is no longer possible; speed is of the essence, although food stores within the body are considerable. Fishing for silver eels is a lucrative occupation on many estuaries. In their haste to reach the sea, some eels even cross land during wet autumn nights, but most pour down rivers. Their sense organs, especially the eyes, lateral lines

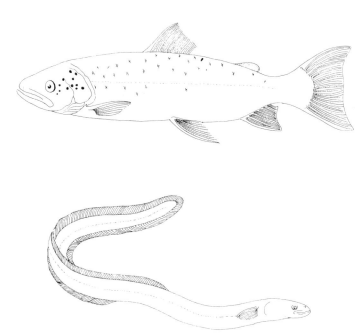

Salmon and eel

and nostrils, are enlarged, no doubt to help in the complex navigation required to reach the breeding grounds – which are probably in the Sargasso sea: 'probably', for it is only assumed, not proved, that all the adults travel to the Sargasso, there to spawn and die. It is from this region that huge numbers of eel larvae, *Leptocephalus*, seem to radiate like ripples from a pebble thrown into water, and it is certainly likely that the breeding area is at the hub of this circle. Sargasso is situated in the western Atlantic, over an area 22–30°N and 48–65°W.

From its first discovery in 1856, *Leptocephalus* confused the scientists, who thought that it was a separate species and it was not until the end of the century that it was recognised as the larval stage of the eel. Johannes Schmidt, a Danish scientist, devoted much of his time to studying this creature between 1906 and 1920, and eventually pinpointed the Sargasso sea as the logical breeding area. He further calculated that the larvae would take something like three years to drift gently on the Gulf Stream to reach Europe. In their last winter before reaching our estuaries they change into what we refer to as elvers; by now they are obviously young eels, though initially their bodies are transparent, so that the skeleton and body organs are clearly visible and the heart's pumping can be observed. On migration upriver they show great ingenuity and no little skill in negotiating eddies and weirs, looking for all the world like animated lengths of string. Naturalists enjoy the sight and fishermen appreciate the bonanza of elvers which adds greatly to their income. Both know that a spring tide will push the fish further upstream, and also that eels are nocturnal, so a spring tide at night in the month of April is likely to produce a good eel run. It is fun to imagine that the incoming eels may well be passing outgoing young salmon hatched at the head of the river. Those which as eggs escaped being eaten by predatory eels will be on their way to fatten and get fit before returning to fresh water to breed themselves.

The Salmon

In studying the salmon (*Salmo salar*) the naturalist is faced with a problem as difficult as that posed by the eel, because though the fresh-water breeding stage can easily be watched, the marine period has proved to be mysterious. We know that a salmon is likely to return to its native river to breed, but how does it recognise home? It seems to do so by chemical means – by a sense of smell or taste, whichever one wants to call it. At one time Britain's rivers abounded with salmon, and it was a food for everyone, not the luxury item that it is today; but such an active fish needs high-quality richly oxygenated water, and pollution as much as, if not more than, over-fishing has been responsible for its accelerating decline.

Life for the salmon begins high up in the gravelly sources of rivers. Spawning occurs in winter, after the incredibly difficult journey upstream against the full flow of the water. Many fish perish as they struggle up torrential waterfalls. A few spent fish, known as kelts, manage to make their way back again to the sea after spawning, and attempt the assault course again in order to breed a second time. Usually the eggs hatch in April, the newly emerged 'alevins' being just over 1.5cm ($\frac{3}{4}$in) long and still retaining a supply of yolk suspended under the body in a sac, which feeds them for a month or so. After that, the fry – or fingerling, as they are now called – must rely on their own hunting abilities. It is a tough initiation and many fail to survive the 'eat but don't be eaten' game. After about a year, the young salmon, their bodies now laterally blotched with black, are referred to as parr. In some southern rivers, particularly the Hampshire Avon, the living is comparatively easy, and on liberal quantities of good food the parr grow quickly to seaworthy condition. Their colour then changes to a shiny silvery sheen, and they are known as grilse. Tagging of Scottish fish has shown that in the more oligotrophic (clear and lacking in food) River Tay the change from parr to grilse may take two or even three years.

May and June seem to be the main departure months for the young salmon, renamed once again and known as smolts. These funnel through the estuaries and out to sea. Once more the value of tagging experiments has been shown, for they have told us that the young salmon grow stout and strong in the plankton-rich waters of the north, especially around Greenland. There they remain usually for some years, though on occasions the return journey may be made after only one year. The returning salmon are now known as grilse.

Though they travel in opposite directions to satisfy their mating urges, salmon and eels face the same problems in adjusting their body fluids to changes in salinity; it may be necessary for them to spend some time in an estuary to allow the body chemistry to adapt. In this sense the estuary is acting in a similar manner to a diver's decompression chamber. An analysis of the body fluids of the salmon shows that the salts in the blood are maintained at a concentration of around 12 per cent of that of sea water. When the fish is swimming in fresh water it will therefore pull in water, by osmosis. To prevent the body from swelling, the large and efficient kidneys work harder and volumes of dilute urine are excreted. In a purely marine habitat, osmotic forces will work in the opposite direction and the fish will tend to dehydrate. To counteract this it drinks quantities of sea water, and can also get rid of excess salt through the gills.

Considerable research, especially by Motais and Maetz in France, has gone into the study of these complex salinity-regulating mechanisms. Using radioactive isotopes, salt molecules have been labelled and traced around the kidney and gill systems. This work has helped to show that most fish are 'stenohaline' (*steno*, narrow, *haline*, salt); that is to say that they can inhabit either salt- or fresh-water habitats but not both. Some fishes, however, are 'eurohaline' (*eury*, wide), much more tolerant of salt levels. Obviously the stickleback, salmon and eel come into this group, but even these are often intolerant of sudden salinity fluctuations. Furthermore immature eels living in fresh water die when placed in sea water; only sexually mature fish are able to cope.

The species so far described are not the only fish found in estuaries. The flounder (*Platichthys flesus*), for example, is able to withstand instantaneous changes from sea water to fresh water, apparently because it has evolved an ingenious method of transferring sodium and chloride ions across its gills. Other fish too pass through the estuarine checkpoint; two species of lamprey, *Lampetra fluviatilis* (the river lamprey) and *Petromyzon marinus* (the sea lamprey), and the sea trout (*Salmo trutta*), all spawn in rivers after they have fattened themselves in the sea.

The sea trout is a distinct variety of the brown trout, which instead of remaining in its natal river makes periodic visits to the sea. It has been possible to demonstrate the value of these 'holidays' by examining the scales on these fish; they show growth patterns that can almost be compared to the annual growth-rings found in trees. The rings on the scales grow thicker during the time spent feeding at sea than when the fish is relying on a diet of fresh-water organisms. As in the closely related salmon, a silver coloration develops just before these trout leave for the sea. Usually later in the same year they return to fresh water, and at this period are referred to as whitlings. This feeding period seems to be an annual event; after the second journey they have earned the anglers' name of sea trout, and a fine sporting fish they are.

The Fishing Birds

As they make their way through the estuary, like other fish such as the dab (*Limanda limanda*), plaice (*Pleuronectes platessa*) and dogfish (*Scyliorhinus canicula*), they must run the gauntlet of predators such as the grey and common seal – which we have already met – and three wonderfully efficient birds. Bobbing about on the flowing tide are the cormorant and the red-breasted merganser, both expert divers, and the grey heron which stalks along with water lapping up to its belly as the tide ebbs, stabbing down at any fish just too late to keep an appointment in the Sargasso or making a return trip from feeding at sea. To watch these experts at work is a great experience: their methods have long been jealously scanned by human anglers. Indeed in parts of the Orient cormorants were trained to dive for fish. They had ropes around their necks so that they could be pulled aboard a boat and rings around their throats so they were unable to swallow the catch. Once the boatman had sufficient for his needs the rings were removed and the cormorant allowed to catch food for itself. In these days of dwindling fish stocks for professional fishermen, not to mention the attraction of amateur angling competitions, any bird which helps itself to a few fish, as these birds must, is certain to earn clamour for its extermination. Fortunately all three species are still thriving, and are in their own particular ways equally fascinating.

The cormorant (*Phalacrocorax carbo*) excels in diving for fish and it must do so efficiently since its feathers are not completely waterproof; the wings are hung out to dry, in typical heraldic posture, for long periods. An estuary is therefore the perfect habitat for it, since as the tide ebbs plenty of exposed mudbanks are available, remaining for a long time as temporary islands, comparatively free from the attacks of predators. Some have suggested that a cormorant standing hunch-backed and wings outspread may not just be drying out its wings, but adopting the posture to help ease down a particularly big fish it has swallowed.

I was once fishing for dabs on a wet January day, the wind sweeping over Morecambe Bay like an avenging demon. There I sat, line held hopefully in a swirling eddy, so cold that I moved hardly at all, when a cormorant flew above my head, turned into the wind, hovered and then landed with a splash just a few metres from me. Suddenly it dived and came up with a flat fish which looked quite large enough to be the famous 'one that got away'. With a twist of the head the fish was turned around and disappeared head-first down the bird's open gullet. No wonder fishermen are jealous! The neat trick of turning the prey before swallowing it is learned early in the life of a fish-eating bird. When a fish is struggling for its life it opens its gill flap (the operculum) and the bird must swallow it head-first so that the cover is pushed closed and it slips down without sticking, a mishap that could be fatal for the bird.

To the estuary-based naturalist, a point of special interest about the cormorant is that it is one of the birds with its own personal desalinating apparatus. Any seabird tends to take in more salt than its kidneys can cope with. Generally speaking the bird kidney will produce urine with salt concentration only about half that of sea water. This impossible situation is brought into balance by the nasal glands, which are situated behind the eyes, which have ducts which open into the nostrils. They can produce a salt solution much more concentrated than brine, and the water left behind can be then used by the bird. The size of the salt gland varies according to the species, the black-headed gull which often breeds inland having comparatively smaller glands than the more marine herring gull. The fresh-water-based tufted duck has much smaller glands than the very closely related marine species, the scaup. Likewise the goosander, which is more of a river bird, has smaller nasal glands than the red-breasted merganser.

The merganser (*Mergus serrator*) is very much an estuary-based species. It breeds mainly in the north and west of Britain, usually very near to the coast though there are increasing numbers of inland breeding records. An interest in the natural world is certainly nothing new, but in the days before efficient binoculars and cameras, the gun was the main tool of the ornithologist – and those of us who complain of the amount of shooting that goes on today would do well to peruse the works of early Victorian ornithologists. The Rev F. O. Morris wrote numerous letters to *The Times* in the 1860s and 1870s complaining about the slaughter then current. His *British Birds*, published in 1857, shows a deep understanding of the distribution of birds. His summary of the status of *Mergus serrator* is a classic example of his craft.

> They frequent the coast, its bays and estuaries, and the lower parts of rivers namely where they disembogue into the sea, but sometime advance upwards, and reach inland waters, though seldom beyond the influence of the tide. . . . In Northumberland these birds occur along the coasts, Holy Island and the Fern Islands [Morris means the Farnes] being favourite localities; also on the shores of Durham. In Lincolnshire the Rev William Waldo Cooper shot one in the Ancholme in the winter of 1853–54. In Northamptonshire the species has occurred on the River Nene. In Suffolk one near Ipswich, as T. J. Wilkinson Esq, of Walsham Hall has written me

Red-breasted merganser with young, photographed from a great distance (Author)

word. In the adjoining county of Norfolk one, a male, an adult bird, was seen at Lowestoft in the third week of July 1852 as recorded by J. H. Gurney Esq, of Easton, in the Zoologist page 3599. In the usual way it is also seen in those parts in the winter months, but old males are seldom obtained except in severe seasons. Many specimens were procured along the coast of Essex and the two last named counties in the winter of 1829–30. They are not uncommon near Yarmouth and generally on Norfolk coast in severe weather, but immature birds are much more common than adult. In Yorkshire, a fine female specimen was shot near Richmond on 12th December 1854; a female also at Barnsley in January of the same year. Some have occurred near Hebden Bridge; also near Doncaster – one in 1837. Individuals too, near York as well as at Huddersfield and at Swillington near Leeds – January 24th 1838 . . . In Cambridgeshire, a pair were shot at Priorwillow, in 1854. A female shot in Burwell Fen, in summer; others have been sold in the Cambridge market. In the sister county of Oxford, a fine specimen of this bird was killed on Otmoor, in February 1838, and in the winter of 1841 two others fell to the gun near Cassington. A pair, male and female, were killed near Reading in 1795. Three were shot, adult birds, a male and two females, at Terrington Marsh, Norfolk on the 7th December, 1849. In Essex two on the Thames near Barking, the beginning of January 1850. In Cornwall one was obtained near Penryn Creek, Falmouth in December 1846 and a second specimen in November 1847; others on the River Truro and its branches. The species has occurred also in Kent, by the Thames, in Worcestershire, on the Severn near Worcester; likewise in Lancashire, Dorsetshire, and Surrey near Chertsey, in November 1842, one was shot out of a flock of thirty-four. In Devonshire it is occasionally procured in immature plumage.

In South Wales Mr. Dillwyn has noticed its occurrence at Swansea. It has also been met with in North Wales. In Montgomeryshire three were seen at Bronafron, on the River Severn January 2nd 1850, of which one was shot. They also breed in Scotland, in Sutherlandshire, on all the lochs, as near Scowrie and elsewhere, likewise in Argyllshire, on Loch Awe, where the nest was found by Sir William Jardine, Bart and Mr. P. J. Selby in June 1828; in Rosshire at Loch Maree, and at East Lothian, more frequent in winter and the like in Caithness. They also remain throughout the year in Orkney, Shetland and the Hebrides and rear their young. Pennant has mentioned their breeding in the Isle of Islay and Mr. Macgillivray found the nest in Harris.

Thus Morris gives us a clear picture of the status of the red-breasted merganser just over a century ago. He goes on to stress that 'These birds are extremely shy and wary, especially during the breeding season.' In view of what he had just written about shooting here, there and almost everywhere, this is hardly surprising. Since Morris's day the species has expanded its range, though it was only in 1950 that breeding was proved in England: eggs were laid at Ravenglass in Cumbria, and since then the Lake District has been well colonised and the bird has spread into Wales.

I once watched a female with fifteen young on the Duddon Estuary, and since eight to ten eggs is the usual clutch I can only assume that this was an example of crèching, one female acting as guardian both to her own young and also to clutches from ducks that are temporarily away feeding or have deserted their young in order to moult. The sea was rough and the animated raft was being carried on a swift current, keeping Mrs Merganser hard at work marshalling all these vulnerable ducklings. I hope that some managed to escape the attentions of the gulls and other predators around, helping to boost the 2,000 pairs which at present breed in Britain – thanks to a climate more suitable for wildfowl breeding than that of a hundred years ago. Our average summers are cooler and winters milder, making long migratory journeys less essential for some birds: more wildfowl have become residents. In winter, however, the population is still enlarged considerably by arrivals from lands to the north and east of Britain.

The diet of the red-breasted merganser, as of the cormorant, contains little that should alarm the fisherman, especially as the population densities are so small. Fish are captured by diving, followed by a rapid pursuit through the water, the bird propelling itself with its webbed feet. It is here that the serrated edge of the bill comes into its own (the merganser is referred to as a 'sawbill', as mentioned below). The 'teeth' slope backwards so that the more the prey struggles the more firmly it is held.

Dabblers, Divers and Sawbills
Ducks can be usefully, though non-scientifically, classified into 'dabblers', including mallard and teal, which obtain their food by grubbing about in shallow water; divers, including scaup and goldeneye, which dive for their food, usually invertebrate, and sawbills, which also dive

but because of their bill structure can take a firm grip on quite large and slippery prey. In Britain we have three species of sawbill – the smew, the goosander and the red-breasted merganser. The smew looks quite different from the others and is much smaller, but although the goosander averages 70cm (28in) and the merganser only 58cm (23in) these two can be confused. Normally the goosander is a fresh-water bird, but in cold weather the estuaries may have both species present. The merganser is of more slender build, and while both females have red heads complete with a straggling crest, the breast of the merganser duck is also reddish, while that of the goosander is creamy-white. The male merganser has this pale breast too, but shares with the goosander a deep green plumage on the head, which at a distance may seem to be black. Again both species are crested.

There are few better occupations for a birdwatcher than spending a whole day watching the tide flow into, and ebb out of, an estuary with cormorants, mergansers, scoters, wigeon, teal, mallards and perhaps a splendid long-tailed duck, rafting along with the prevailing current. As the sea recedes the swimming ducks are replaced by the graceful wading heron, king of the shallow-water hunters.

The Heron

The history of the heron (*Ardea cinerea*) is one of the most chequered in the annals of British ornithology. In the days of falconry it was a favourite quarry species and often appeared on the menu of the privileged classes. As befits a blue-riband bird it was given protection in order to preserve stocks. Always envied by the greedy fisherman, Old Nog, as the heron was often called, was believed to possess magical powers which attracted fish. Some were sure that the magic was contained in the legs; a dead heron was eagerly sought, and the skin stripped from its shanks and mixed into the fisherman's bait, in the hope that the spell would rub off!

The species reached a low ebb when the sport of hawking fell into decline; the subsequent loss of protection, plus the increasing efficiency and availability of fire-arms, meant problems for a bird that breeds in conspicuous colonies and had few remaining friends. Although the majority of breeding birds prefer the company of others, and 99 per cent prefer to nest in trees, there are occasional pairs happy in their own company; some of these 'anti-social' herons raise their young on cliff faces or on the drier spots amidst marshlands. It was these small pockets of nonconformist breeders that prevented herons being wiped out in some areas where persecution of the colonial sites was ruthless.

Elsewhere, especially in privately owned woods, some heronries have been in use for centuries. A census of heronries of the British Isles has been conducted since 1928 and is now controlled by that efficient body

Grey heron

the British Trust for Ornithology. The population appears to have fluctuated between just over 2,000 and just under 5,000 breeding pairs, the troughs following bad winters, especially those of the 1940s and 1962–3. During any winter, but particularly a cold one, there will be a seawards movement, since salt water has a much lower freezing point and will continue to offer good fishing in sub-zero temperatures. Eels figure largely in the diet and many a battle-royal takes place between a writhing desperate fish and a hungry determined heron. If the prey is of any significant size the heron takes it, walking slowly with a prancing stiff-legged strut, to a solid patch, and proceeds to bash it on the ground, occasionally stabbing downwards with its daggerlike bill before picking

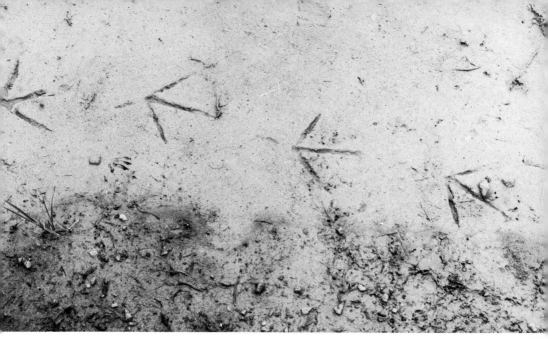

Heron footprints on mudflats (Author)

up the weakening eel and making another attempt to swallow it. In the end the eel is overcome, but not before its adversary has become covered in slime and blood which if allowed to dry on the feathers would greatly reduce both their waterproofing qualities and their flying efficiency. So the heron family have evolved an ingenious mechanism for dealing with this problem. Some of the feathers on the flanks and breast gradually break down, to produce what is known as powder down; this is plucked and rubbed on to the slime-laden feathers, soaking up the moisture. Furthermore one of the toes has evolved a comblike structure which is used to scrape off the powder with the accompanying slime. In a surprisingly short time the heron is cleaned up and ready for a bath and another meal. Fishing continues until the tide has ebbed, when the heron flies off for a quiet roost.

Ecological Niches

Life on the estuary is equally intense when the tide is out, for beneath the mud lurks a host of living organisms, fuel which fires the whole complex food-web of the estuary: masses of worms, molluscs, crustaceans and other invertebrates, a topic discussed in Chapter 6. And the exposed mudflats are rich in almost uniformly distributed food for birds, with little cover available for predators. Many different species gather here at low-tide periods, especially in winter when pressures imposed by the breeding season are forgotten, particularly the Charadriiformes – waders, gulls and terns. Waders are a large collection of mostly long-legged birds which obtain their food by probing their

55

bills down into the mud. A wader's bill is anything but a dead insensitive structure; it is often covered by a delicate tissue rich in nerve-endings, enabling the bird to recognise food items.

There is a biological principle that no two species can share the same habitat and eat identical food without one species having a marginal advantage over the other; that one will have a greater chance of survival and slowly, but surely, the less well-endowed must either modify its habits or become extinct. Thus each species develops its own ecological niche. Nowhere is this principle better demonstrated than by looking at the length and shape of the bills of waders. The long curved bill of the curlew can push deeper in search of food than the redshank, which in turn has longer legs and a longer bill than the ringed plover and can wade into puddles to reach prey not available to its smaller competitor; but the ringed plover is well satisfied to take the smaller fry left by the larger birds. Over centuries of time each species has evolved its own feeding niche and they can all dine together without competition or getting in each other's way.

Bill and leg lengths of waders
Observations made at Morecambe Bay, Cumbria, March 1981. Measurements taken from the *Handbook of British Birds* (Witherby et al., 1942)

Bird	Bill length (mm)	Leg length (mm)
Curlew	100–152	66–80
Bar-tailed godwit	72–106	46–51
Redshank	38–44	44–50
Knot	30–38	27–31
Dunlin	25–34	21–25
Sanderling	23–28	22–26
Grey plover	27–32	43–50
Turnstone	20–24	23–26
Ringed plover	14–16	25–28

The prey species too have their own ecological niche, as nature plays her game of check and checkmate. The tiny snail *Hydrobia*, fed upon by the ringed plover, lives near the surface; the lugworms (*Arenicola* spp) are able to burrow deep into the mud, and when the tide is out they can only be reached by the long probing bills of the curlew and perhaps the bar-tailed godwit. On the Lune estuary, near Lancaster, I made a list of the species of wader feeding on the mudflats.

The Oyster-catcher
By far the most numerous species was the delightful oyster-catcher

(*Haematopus ostralegus*), which feeds in dense and very aggressive masses on the cockle (*Cerastoderma edule*); it had no need to worry about competitors, for all other species, including the gulls, kept well out of the way. In other parts of Morecambe Bay the oyster-catcher feeds greedily on the mussel (*Mytilus edule*). In fact one shellfish it does not regularly eat is the oyster (*Ostrea edulis*), which is perhaps just as well because the poor bird is unpopular enough with the mollusc fishermen as it is. We could usefully dispense with the name oyster-catcher and revert to the older and much more appropriate name of sea-pie. No doubt because of its occasional devastating attacks on valuable cockle and mussel beds (valuable to man, I should stress), this bird's food has been studied in detail in recent years. During 1957 and 1958, Drinnan investigated the feeding rates of Morecambe Bay oyster-catchers, and found that each bird could consume between 14 and 51 cockles per hour; this could, depending on the size of cockle, result in a daily intake of between 214 and 315!

Some British oyster-catchers breed on the seashore, preferring shingle beaches (see Chapter 4), but in recent years they have shown an increasing tendency to nest inland, along the shingle banks of rivers; sewage works and moors are also becoming more attractive. This is due in part to the sea-pie's increase in population, but the main reason is the increasing number of holidaymakers wandering along its traditional breeding areas.

In winter the population is swelled by massive southward migrations from the ice-bound breeding grounds in Iceland and the Faeroes, although ringing has shown that some birds which hatched in Britain may winter in southern Spain. The ringers have also proved that Morecambe Bay is a favoured wintering ground, some birds returning year after year. Huge flocks can build up, often exceeding 40,000 individuals at times of migration from August to October; but the wintering population is probably about 75 per cent of this figure. Again Drinnan's work throws some light on the behaviour of these flocks. He used aerial photography to establish that the population of oyster-catchers in the area of Cartmel Wharf was in the order of 30,000 during the winter of 1954–5. His figures suggested that the flock would have eaten 22 per cent of the cockle population during that winter. We must take care, however, not to make generalised statements and to avoid being panicked into wholesale cullings, since cyclic fluctuations are very much part of nature's scheme; and the 1954–5 figures might well be a peak, to be followed by a trough in the fortunes of the oyster-catchers.

3
Saltmarshes

Here a grave flora scarcely deigns to bloom
Nor wears a rosy bloom, nor sheds perfume:
The few dull flowers that o'er the place are spread
Partake the nature of their fenny bed.

The Victorian poet Crabbe wrote freely on natural themes and showed a rare grasp of his subject, keeping remarkably free from 'poetic licence'. Only qualified agreement with this poem relating to saltmarsh flora is possible, however. Certainly very few species have evolved strategies of sufficient ingenuity to ensure survival in this habitat; but the word dull is hardly fair. The pink of thrift, the blues of sea aster and sea lavender, contrast delightfully with the admittedly dull grey-yellow of the purslane, while the succulent green leaves of scurvy grass serve to highlight the sparkling white four-petalled flowers. If you take the time to search beneath the dominant plants you will find the small delicate blooms of sea milkwort and the sea spurreys.

Almost all plants found in saltmarshes are 'halophytes', *hals* being the Greek word for salt. They have a specialised cell structure and a highly adapted chemistry which enable them not only to cope with growing in a salty substrate but also to withstand regular immersion in brine. They still have problems in employing a plant's normal method of osmosis to obtain water, as it is clearly not possible for the cell sap to be at a higher concentration than sea water. The strategy is to take in water at times when the ground water is at its least salty – during periods of heavy rain, when the tide is out. After that, what we have we hold; hence most of the plants are succulents, full of spongy aqueous tissue whose water supply can be drawn on at times when the salt concentration of the substrate is high.

There are many reasons why saltmarshes fascinate the naturalist, one being the high counts of wildfowl. The aspiring botanist can gain confidence in flower identification, since there are so few species to get to know. Those who like their natural history to be systematic will find the saltings show distinct zonation; the best way to see this is to follow the ebbing tide (this will ensure that there is no danger of being drowned by the advancing sea). At the point where marsh and sea regularly merge the early development can be studied. If we begin at this point and follow an imaginary route back from the sea to the land, pausing to study each zone until finally arriving at the solid grazing land, we can understand how land is naturally reclaimed from the sea.

The Early Stages

The first sign that the formation of a saltmarsh may be possible is an accumulation of green algae on the mud; species of *Ulothrix*, *Enteromorpha* and *Vaucheria* will be prominent. It is here too that the first flowering plant may be found, and this is eel grass (*Zostera* spp), sometimes called grass wrack. There are three very similar species, all of which are perennials with long grassy leaves and creeping stems. The flowers are green and small, enclosed in a hollow sheaf at the base of the leaves. Pollination takes place under water which is probably the main evolutionary reason for *Zostera*'s success in an environment so hostile for flowering plants. The smallest of the three species is *Zostera nana* – the small eel grass – but it is by far the toughest in ability to cope with exposure. Then comes *Zostera hornemanniana* which was only fully described and separated from *Zostera marina* by Tutin in 1936. Its main distinguishing features are the notches at the ends of its leaves, which are not present in *Zostera marina*; the leaves are also considerably narrower. *Zostera marina* is the largest of the three and is widely distributed around the coast, especially in East Anglia and southern England, where it often forms huge meadows which do much to prepare the muddy substratum for the next of the colonists, usually annual glassworts (*Salicornia* spp). The flowering period of the eel grasses is fairly long; it can begin as early as June and go on well into September although the peak is mid-August, at which time the long green leaves can reach a full metre in length.

During the 1930s a killer disease hit eel grass both in western Europe and along the eastern seaboard of North America, and many mudbanks which were only held together by the plant's root systems began to erode so dramatically that important shipping lanes were threatened by severe silting. There has been a slow recovery since then but it is still not back to its former glory. The collection of eel-grass leaves, which are tough but flexible, and were used for packing delicate merchandise such as china and glass, was once a profitable industry; and the wet leaves were excellent fertiliser. To wildlife the loss was an even worse disaster.

No species was affected as badly as the Brent goose, perhaps the most marine of all geese with well-developed nasal glands (see Chapter 2). During their breeding period in the high Arctic they feed on grass and moss, while in winter they depend largely upon *Enteromorpha* and eel grass. The feeding rhythm is determined by tide times and the geese

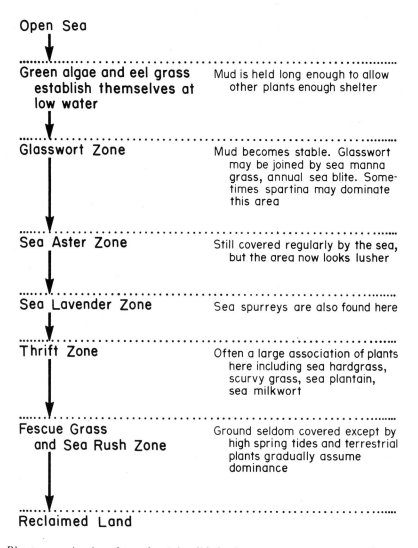

Open Sea

↓

Green algae and eel grass establish themselves at low water — Mud is held long enough to allow other plants enough shelter

↓

Glasswort Zone — Mud becomes stable. Glasswort may be joined by sea manna grass, annual sea blite. Sometimes spartina may dominate this area

↓

Sea Aster Zone — Still covered regularly by the sea, but the area now looks lusher

↓

Sea Lavender Zone — Sea spurreys are also found here

↓

Thrift Zone — Often a large association of plants here including sea hardgrass, scurvy grass, sea plantain, sea milkwort

↓

Fescue Grass and Sea Rush Zone — Ground seldom covered except by high spring tides and terrestrial plants gradually assume dominance

↓

Reclaimed Land

Plant succession in saltmarshes (simplified scheme)

know when the feeding grounds will be uncovered – yet another example of the presence of a biological clock, already mentioned in connection with the shore crab. In the hard days of winter the birds may be too hungry to wait for the tide completely to ebb away, and desperately up-end in shallow water, tugging at the rooted eel grass. It was, therefore, only to be expected that the Brent's population would be drastically reduced when the eel grass perished. One area which remained fairly rich in *Zostera* was the marshes at Foulness in Essex, which is why naturalists, already concerned about the problems of the geese, were so opposed to the suggested construction of an airport there. The danger of collisions with geese was another reason to drop the plan, since Brent geese are strongly attached to their traditional wintering areas.

Ironically, just as the eel grass began to recover, even the conservative Brents were beginning to change their diet and had begun to move inland to sample the root crops in the fields, much to the chagrin of the local farmers. They made short work of both grasses and root crops – after all they have enough centuries of evolutionary muscle behind them to be able to deal with the toughest of roots. Eel grass is now again growing in many of the traditional habitats and the Brents soon fill any empty niches.

The Glasswort Zone

Continuing from the *Zostera* fields towards the land, we approach the area which many would regard as the first zone of the real saltmarsh: the glasswort zone. Glasswort, or sea samphire, is in fact a complex of slightly differing species. They are difficult to separate, but the most dominant is usually *Salicornia herbacea*, marsh samphire. The first colonisers, a few isolated plants, are liable to be uprooted by wave action, and this is why some shelter from the open sea, however slight, is always needed before a saltmarsh can become established. Piers,

Glasswort growing in the Duddon estuary (Author)

groynes and even the wrecks of stranded ships can provide this essential protection. Gradually the roots gather quantities of mud and silt and bind them together, but the zone of the marsh dominated by glasswort usually has patches of bare ground between the isolated plants. The grass *Glyceria maritima* begins to thrive once glasswort has provided some stability; algae, too, may find an ideal vacant niche here. *Salicornia* is a very succulent plant, flowering from July to September and can grow up to 30cm (12in). It has no recognisable leaves, but the jointed stems are green and make food as leaves do, by the process of photosynthesis. The inconspicuous flowers, in groups of three, shrink into a protective fold of a spike which originates from a joint. At one time the plant was burned to produce soda, used in glassmaking, and in some parts, especially on the Wyre estuary, the stems are still gathered to make a pickle to eat with beef sandwiches. Moving inland through the glasswort zone, other plants begin to appear, including annual seablite and sea aster.

This progression is typical of most saltmarsh developments, but there is the odd occasion when other species take on the role of pioneer-plant. On the west coast, sea manna grass (*Puccinellia maritima*) may appear before or at the same time as glasswort. This seems to be because the manna grass prefers sandy areas to mud, and west-coast estuaries tend to be much sandier than those on the east coast. This is the commonest of the saltmarsh grasses, but it can also be found growing on cliff ledges, particularly in Scotland. It can quickly produce smooth lawns of sea-washed turf, which sheep – often to their cost – find irresistible. The plant grows from a perennial rootstock, producing fleshy leaves which are rolled inwards. The stems trail along the ground and are able to put down roots, a most useful attribute for a flowering plant. The flowers, appearing from July to September, are carried on a prominent stem which can be more than 30cm high.

There are other areas, especially on the south coast, such as around Southampton and Poole Harbour, where the mud is so thick, deep and mobile that the rather small *Salicornia* plants are totally swamped. It is in such areas that the tall, powerful, rice or cord grass (*Spartina townsendii*) thrives. This plant is a good demonstration of what biologists refer to as hybrid vigour. When two plants are crossed, very occasionally a new plant is produced which inherits the strengths of both parents with none of their weaknesses. What is now referred to as *Spartina townsendii* is in fact a hybrid between mat grass (*Spartina stricta*) a European species, and *Spartina alternifolia* from America. The hybrid was first recorded from Southampton Water in 1870 and from that time its spread has been dramatic, although it has been assisted by deliberate plantings in attempts to stabilise estuarine mud close to important ports.

Spartina townsendii *growing near Sunderland Point* (Author)

Spartina *in Borth saltmarsh, near Aberystwyth* (Alan W. Heath)

Spartina townsendii is much larger than *Spartina stricta*, which is still found in some saltmarshes. Underground roots dig deeply into the mud and anchor the plant, while others spread horizontally to cover a large area, soaking up minerals and water. Above the mud a stout stem carries stiff, erect leaves searching for light, waving about in the tidal eddies. The plants trap silt, which builds up rapidly; *Spartina* can reclaim land from the sea quicker than any other species. It tends to become so dominant that few other species can coexist with it – only the odd plant of glasswort and sea aster.

Whatever the initial dominant species may be, the marsh eventually stabilises sufficiently for other species to find it attractive and take over from the pioneer. The next zone of the marsh may be dominated by sea manna grass, already described, but the most obvious dominant is nearly always the sea aster.

The Sea Aster Zone

A thorough survey of an area of marsh at Scolt Head (made by Chapman in 1934) found that sea aster (*Aster tripolium*) had replaced glasswort, which had only managed to hang on in a few bare areas of

Pintail, a duck which winters in the shallow seas around saltmarshes and estuaries (Author)

mud. Also present was the European cord grass and annual seablite. The latter (*Suaeda maritima*) is an interesting plant to look at and although never dominant in its own right is present on many salt-marshes, including those at the heads of sea lochs in Scotland. The flowering period is from July to late October or even early November; though most plants are quite small, a height of over 50cm (20in) can be reached. A smooth, slender and straggling stem carries fleshy pale green leaves which slowly change to a pleasant red as autumn advances. In the axils of the leaves, especially in September, small clusters of green flowers will be seen.

Carter, working on the Thames estuary at Canvey Island in the early 1930s, noticed that in the zone dominated by sea aster there also grew quite extensive patches of green algae, which are of course only simple seaweeds. He found *Ulothrix flacca* dominant in the winter months, replaced by *Enteromorpha prolifera* in spring and summer. *Enteromorpha* means 'resembling the form of intestines', a good description of this plant which looks a bit like unravelled sausage skins with a green tinge. I have noted all these species on the saltmarshes of Morecambe Bay and the estuary of Wordsworth's beloved River Duddon. Many of these plants are attractive food items for birds, and species such as sea aster and thrift produce nutritious seeds which are eagerly sought by large numbers of wintering wildfowl, including wigeon and teal. These two ducks themselves are possible food for the ever-alert peregrine, now alas something of a rarity, but they will be found on most saltmarshes during winter.

Wigeon

This is a very gregarious species. The drakes are easily recognised both by sight and sound, though the duller duck as usual presents a more difficult identification problem. The head of the male is of a delightful chestnut colour, with an obvious custard-yellow streak on the forehead. He also has a patch of white on the wing, clearly visible in flight. His plaintive whistle is another feature not possessed by his mate. She, however, looks pleasant enough, her upper parts delicately mottled in a rich shade of chestnut.

Like the Brent goose, wigeon were affected by the reduction in eel grass, but they proved to be more quickly resourceful and began to feed in other zones of the saltmarsh; where these proved inadequate they moved to inland sites. This drift was encouraged in the area of the Ouse Washes by the development of reserves, particularly by the Wildfowl Trust and the RSPB. So successful has this been that the area now supports more wintering wigeon than any other European site, the population having risen from about 5,000 in the mid-1960s to a January peak that often exceeds 40,000 birds. Given a choice, however, the wigeon is still a saltmarsh bird, and is one of the most prized quarries of

65

the wildfowler, since its flesh is so palatable. The days of the punt gunner and the decoy trap are now mercifully gone for ever, but many folk still enjoy spending a winter's dawn stalking the wary wigeon through the oozing, often stinking and always sticky, mud so typical of the saltings. The photographer also enjoys the primitive thrill of the stalk, often interrupted by an explosive crack of wings as a spring of teal, an even more elusive species than the wigeon, rises from the muddy creeks of the marsh.

The Teal

At 40cm (16in), the teal (*Anas crecca*) is some 10cm (4in) shorter than the wigeon. Substantial numbers (about 5,000 pairs) breed in Britain, but many thousands more pour in during the winter. The shallow waters and marshy pools typical of saltmarshes are ideal habitat, and the teal's bill is perfectly adapted to sieve out nutritious seeds and the prolific tiny snail Hydrobia. The snail is also taken by the shelduck, which frequents saltmarshes and also sandy shores (Chapter 6). Being small and meaty, teal have to run the gauntlet of many avian predators including the greater black-backed gull, merlin and peregrine which is probably the reason why they prefer to feed at night. Just as the drake wigeon's custard-coloured flash on the forehead can be seen at a distance even in poor light, so the yellow line running from the drake teal's bill over and around the eye, and a second yellow line below the orbit, can be seen easily, as can the equally bright yellow patch on the rump.

To sieve food in shallow water the bird frequently upends, thus exposing the rump and enabling the observer to identify it. As with wigeon, both sexes will be in the flock, but the drakes are larger than the ducks, and the proportion of them present provides a classic example of Bergmann's Rule – that there is a tendency for the body-size of a warm-blooded species, or even a sub-species, to increase as the temperature decreases. So the further north you go in our hemisphere, the more likely you are to find slightly larger individuals of a given species. This is because large bodies conserve heat better, since they have a larger volume compared to their surface area which loses heat to the environment. In mixed flocks of teal there tends to be an increasing proportion of males as you move northwards.

The winter birdwatcher is more likely to see a hunting peregrine over saltmarshes than anywhere else, and the presence of this graceful killer brings a sense of dread to all birds which rise in panic-stricken flocks and fly about calling in disorientated confusion, making it easier for the predator to select its meal. Once – but an unforgettable once – I saw this happen just after dawn on the Solway marshes. The tide ebbed slowly, bird calls echoed through the mist; finally the weak winter sun punched holes in the watery film and revealed the splendid sight of massed birds feeding before the backdrop of the Galloway hills. Suddenly the birds stopped grazing, raised their heads almost as one, and then scattered into the air. Wings cracked, frantic calls mingled one into the other, and a group of eight panic-stricken black-headed gulls, slow to rise, headed for the Cumbrian hills. At first I could not see the reason for all this haste until out of the sun, like any good fighter-pilot, came a female peregrine hellbent on breakfast. As she pulled out of her 45° dive she seemed to be passing through the gulls, when she reached out with a lazy-looking claw; the thud as she struck the unlucky victim was clearly audible. Feathers flew everywhere and within seconds of the headless corpse crashing on to the soft mud the peregrine falcon, the latter word referring specifically to the female, was feeding upon the choice bits.

The male peregrine is usually known as the tiercel, indicating that he is one-third smaller than his mate. The female is also darker than the male, but both have a moustachial stripe, and the adults have yellow eye-ring and legs – slate-blue in immature birds. The population of peregrines fell during the 1939–45 war when many were killed in case they interfered with homing pigeons carrying messages. The situation had just begun to improve when an even greater threat crept up. Beginning in the early 1950s the breeding populations of peregrines and other birds of prey fell dramatically, due it was eventually discovered to the use on farmland of very persistent pesticides, particularly aldrin and dieldrin. These have been proved to affect the whole breeding cycle, in particular causing the females to lay eggs with shells so thin that even the weight of the incubating birds may break them. Pressure from conservationists has resulted in the poisons being banned, but it takes time for such substances to work their way through all the complex biological pathways. Eventually the peregrine population slowly began to recover, and hopefully this situation will continue and the watcher on the saltings will occasionally be thrilled by the sight of this magnificent bird. The balance of nature can only be kept by retaining top predators.

The Sea Lavender Zone

There will be plenty for a peregrine to eat distributed throughout a saltmarsh, not least in the next zone to be described, which at low tide is often brimming and bubbling with passerines feeding on the seeds of plants such as the dominant sea lavender. Prominent birds here include greenfinches, yellowhammers, linnets and meadow pipits (*Anthus pratensis*).

This is the zone of the sea lavender (*Limonium vulgare*), which is at its colourful best in summer and early autumn. Some marshes, those around the Dovey in Wales for example, lack sea lavender but this is

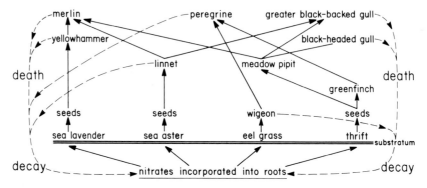

Food web of a typical saltmarsh

almost certainly due to heavy grazing by sheep. A fleshy perennial, it has purple flowers on stems 15–30cm (6in–1ft); they have a weaker aroma than the common lavender in our gardens but despite this add significantly to the delight of the saltings. They are often dried and used for decoration in winter, and our ancestors used the seeds as a remedy for dysentery.

Other Plants of the Sea Lavender Zone

In 1918 Heslop-Harrison made an intensive study of the Tees and found that sea manna grass (*Puccinellia maritima*) was co-dominant with sea lavender, but also present were a few blooms of sea aster, sea plantain, annual seablite, sea arrowgrass and two sea spurreys. Sea arrowgrass (*Triglochin maritima*) arises from a tough perennial rhizome anchored firmly in the marsh. The slender but very fleshy leaves can grow up to half a metre (18in) in length. The stout plantain-like flowering stem can reach a height of 60cm (2ft), the top third bearing a slender spike of yellowish-green flowers, which can be found in bloom as early as April and as late as November.

The sea spurreys (*Spergularia salina*, the lesser sea spurrey, and *Spergularia marginata*, the greater) are attractive little five-petalled pale pinkish flowers, with fleshy leaves paired along the branching, trailing stems. In the August saltmarsh the spurreys are often hidden beneath the almost smothering foliage of the dominant plants, but the leaves seem to manage to obtain enough light to carry on essential photosynthetic activities. A third species, the rock or cliff sea spurrey (*Spergularia rupicola*), is confined to rocks and cliffs, but the other two are found together on many saltmarshes.

The lesser sea spurrey occurs in both annual and biennial forms, its prostrate stems often entangled around the stouter growths of sea lavender, which it uses as a prop as it searches for essential light. It has a deep pink flower, 1.2cm ($\frac{1}{2}$in) across, the petals being shorter than the sepals. The lesser sea spurrey flowers from June to September.

The greater sea spurrey has a pale pink flower with white centre, 1.5–2.4cm ($\frac{3}{4}$–1in) across, with the petals the same length as the sepals. This spurrey is a perennial, and again it flowers from June to September. If the August saltmarsh is dominated by the plants of the middle regions, such as sea lavender and sea aster, then the month of May is the time of the thrift zone, which as we continue our inland stroll gradually takes over dominance from the sea lavender.

The Thrift Zone

The zone of the thrift or sea-pink (*Armeria maritima*) typically consists of close, lush-looking turf. Thrift cannot tolerate very high salt concentrations, as can be seen by its vigorous growth if plants are transplanted into inland gardens – a practice which despite the fact that it has no medicinal value has gone on since at least the fifteenth century. It is, however, extremely tolerant of grazing sheep, no doubt due to the fact that it grows from compact rosettes. The leaves are fleshy, long and flat, and the small rose-coloured flowers are closely packed together in round heads on single stalks. Below each head is a whorl of scale-like bracts, and these together with the funnel-shaped calyx (this is the collective name for the sepals) remain long after the flower has died, looking just like strips of thin brown paper. Over the course of centuries thrift has had a number of vernacular names, including sea-daisy, pin-cushion, cushion-pink, but my favourite is the Gaelic *tonn a chladaich*, beach wave.

Also present in the thrift zone are sea milkwort, sea plantain, sea arrowgrass and sea hard grass (*Parapholis strigosa*), the latter having an interesting distribution pattern: it is abundant in the Mediterranean, still manages to thrive in southern England but gradually becomes less common as you journey northwards. Hard grass is an annual plant but each year puts out a much-branched stem reaching 15–30cm (6in–1ft) in height, producing a curved flowering spike between August and October. Another, stouter, species of hard grass (*Parapholis incurva*) often flowers as early as June but is restricted to south-western England.

Scurvy Grass
A plant which is not so restricted begins to make a prominent claim to a place on the marsh at this level: the fascinating and formerly valuable scurvy grass (*Cochlearia officinalis*), which was a much-used plant in the times of the apothecary's shop: and with reason this time. Modern extraction techniques prove that the plant contains an oil which is full of vitamin C, and many a sailor must have blessed it for keeping him

free from scurvy, that plague of badly fed ancient mariners. Hakluyt in his *Voyages* described the symptoms: 'The gums were loosed, swolne, and exulcerate; the mouth grievously stinking; the thighs and legs are withall verre often full of blewe spots, not much unlike those that came of bruses; the face and the rest of the bodie is often times of a pale colour; and the feet are swolne, as in the dropsie.' A fair description of the disease, which affects the blood vessels and causes internal bleeding. Before fresh fruit and vegetables were available throughout the year, scurvy-grass medicines were brewed up for land dwellers too, the bitter taste being moderated by the addition of liberal doses of spices. The plant even had its own street cry, a feature of Tudor England:

> Hay'ny wood to cleave,
> Will you buy any scurvy grass?
> Will you buy any glasses
> Of ripe St Thomas onions?

Crops of it were grown in the physic garden, but there was good money to be had by collecting the wild plant from the saltmarshes around the Thames estuary. Gradually scurvy grass went out of fashion as pleasanter-tasting fresh fruits from abroad began first to trickle and then flood into the markets. Even the traditionally conservative British Navy took to providing its crews with fresh limes for their vitamin C, earning us the name of 'limey', which the whole nation is now saddled with. But what does scurvy grass look like and which birds share its habitat? There are actually four species of the plant, all members of the cruciferae family, their flowers being made up of four petals arranged in the form of a cross. They are summarised opposite.

Saltmarsh dominated by sea purslane, Holkham, Norfolk (P. Wakely/Nature Conservancy Council)

British Scurvy Grasses

	DISTRIBUTION	PREFERRED HABITAT	LIFE CYCLE	FLOWERING PERIOD	LEAF SHAPE	FLOWERS	SEED PODS
Common scurvy grass (*Cochlearia officinalis*)	Common throughout	Saltmarshes, cliffs	Perennial	April–July	Lower leaves kidney-shaped, long-stalked; upper leaves stalkless and narrower	White, tinged purple. 1cm ($\frac{2}{5}$in)	Globular
Long-leaved scurvy grass (*Cochlearia anglica*)	Chiefly south, rare in Scotland	Muddy estuaries and saltmarshes. Occasionally cliffs	Usually biennial	May–June	Narrow and clasp the stem	White, 2cm ($\frac{4}{5}$in)	Oval-oblong up to 2cm ($\frac{4}{5}$in)
Stalked scurvy grass, or early scurvy grass (*Cochlearia danica*)	More common in south. Rare in Scotland	Cliffs, sea walls, muddy estuaries, very occasionally sand dunes	Annual	March–August	All stalked and ivy-shaped	White/purple 0.75cm (0.3in)	Oval
Scottish scurvy grass (*Cochlearia scotica*)	Rare Arctic plant confined to North Scotland and Ireland	Shingle, sand, occasionally rocks. Not a saltmarsh plant	Biennial	June–September	Stalked, kidney-shaped	Very small	Oval

All the zones so far discussed are clearly distinguishable in many marshes, but in others the areas merge together, forming what is technically known as a 'general saltmarsh community'. Nowhere is this better demonstrated than at Scolt Head in Norfolk, where there are no fewer than six co-dominants: thrift, sea manna grass, sea lavender, sea arrowgrass, sea purslane and even the lesser sea spurrey. It seems that the plants are not in direct competition, since their roots penetrate to different depths; thus each has its own ecological niche, a similar situation to that of the feeding waders discussed in Chapter 2. Cold and windswept in winter, these areas have a carpet of flowers in summer.

Marshland Geese
Whatever the make-up of these saltings there is ample and varied food for wildfowl. Several species of geese make use of them from October to April. The Wildfowl Trust, well aware of this, has been largely responsible for halting the decline of barnacle geese on the Solway and pink-footed geese on the Southport marshes, and for stabilising the population of white-fronted geese on the Severn estuary. The Trust has reserves at Caerlaverock on Solway, Martin Mere, Southport and Slimbridge on the Severn, ensuring that a constant watch is kept on the vulnerable populations. A naturalist paying regular visits to salt-marshes needs to become familiar with these species as well as the Brent goose discussed earlier in this chapter, for they may visit almost any estuary at times of bad weather during their immigration periods. During the winter of 1962–3, for example, the Duddon estuary at Foxfield carried both pink-footed and barnacle geese as well as 300 greylag geese, 80 mute swans and 50 Bewick's swans. The mute swans regularly flighted in from their inland roosts which were frozen solid, the drone of their wings echoing over the frozen marshes as they planed down to feed on *Enteromorpha* at the seaward end of the marsh. The greylags and barnacles had almost certainly been driven down from Scotland, probably from the Solway, and on one never-to-be-forgotten day there were over 20,000 birds on the move, probably the whole of the Solway population.

In fact there are three discrete populations of barnacle geese (*Branta leucopsis*). A group of about 50,000 birds breed in Russia and winter in the Netherlands; and a group of Greenland breeders, numbering some 20,000, winter on Islay, off western Scotland. This population has shown a dramatic increase since the 1950s, when the counts were often below 3,000. Then there is what is known as the Svalbard breeding population, mainly centred upon Spitzbergen, which is the main island of the archipelago: these are the birds that winter on the Solway. Workers from the Wildfowl Trust have made regular counts for many years and have seen the population rise from about 300 in 1948–9 to

White-fronted goose – large flocks winter on the Severn (Author)

Barnacle goose – bird of the saltings (Author)

Goose barnacles on a North Devon beach (Leslie Jackman/Wildlife Picture Agency)

over 7,000 in 1976–7. A surprising fact is that although Islay is only 170km (110 miles) from Caerlaverock as the barnacle flies, the two populations remain absolutely distinct.

Wintering geese require fairly short grass, since their bills, although strong, are fairly short; thus saltmarshes grazed by sheep throughout the summer are ideal. Contrary to some suggestions, barnacle geese do not eat barnacles – nor have any other connection with them! In the Middle Ages, it was often stated that the geese developed from goose barnacles (*Lepas anatifera*): when these crustaceans are feeding, their filtering apparatus looks superficially like the neck of a goose! It was believed by many that the goose wriggled out of the barnacle shell and then quickly grew in size during the winter before flying away, no one knew where, in the spring. Perhaps those who put about this strange story had some method in their apparent madness. In a Catholic country, meat was not allowed on the menu on Fridays, nor during Lent or on certain saints' days; and perhaps this bird could be classed as a fish? This must be the reason that the legend was allowed to continue!

Both barnacle and pink-footed geese worry farmers with land adjoining the saltings when they visit their crops in hungry flocks. They certainly take the stolons of clovers, which may reduce the fertility of the land, but they do at least put something back by way of their droppings. They are only now and then guilty of substantial damage. For example, though pink-feet (*Anser brachyrhynchus*) are often accused of eating potatoes, an item which has only figured in their diet

74

since about 1880, what they actually eat are the chopped-up useless pieces left by the harvesting machinery. Indeed the geese may well prevent a build-up of insect pests of potatoes by removing these potential overwintering sites.

Like the barnacle geese the pink-feet have distinct populations, but this time concentrated in only two regions. The Svalbard population, which winters in Denmark and Holland, has remained static at about 16,000 birds. The Icelandic population winters in Britain, and according to Ogilvie and Boyd (1976) was in the order of 30,000 in 1950–51 but had peaked at 89,000 in 1974–5. The Solway is an important estuary for much of this population, as are the Southport marshes, and with such a rapid increase it is no wonder that some farmers complain when they watch the geese descending into their fields like locusts; they must feel even worse when only the green tops of their valuable crops peep above the snow level. During a normal winter, however, the natural productivity of the saltings provides sufficient food to support the goose population, and the farmers need not worry.

The Fescue Zone

Fescue is much commoner on west-coast estuaries, often occurring as a co-dominant with sea manna grass on the seaward side and with the mud rush on the other. Its main strength is its ability to cope both with immersion in sea water and with long periods of desiccation. Associated with this zone are, again, the sea arrowgrass, thrift, sea hard grass and sea milkwort, with buck's-horn plantain (*Plantago coronopus*), the leaves of which are shaped like a fallow deer's antlers; and especially frequent is the sea plantain (*Plantago maritima*), which on some east-coast marshes may be plentiful enough to form its own zone. It seems to be a great favourite with sheep, so much so that in North Wales attempts were made to cultivate it commercially. Sea plantain is a perennial, the long narrow leaves arising from a branched rootstock. The flowering period is protracted from late May to late October, the blooms being carried on long stalks. The most prominent feature of the flowers are the delicate yellow stamens.

Coming to the final stages in the reclamation of land from the sea, we enter the highest zones of the saltmarsh, which are usually dominated by red fescue (*Festuca rubra*) and finally by rushes, the sea rush and the mud rush.

The Sea-rush Zone

Eventually the fescue and/or sea plantain give way to the dominant plants of the final zone, that of the sea rush. There may be either of two dominants here: the sea rush (*Juncus maritimus*) or the less common and smaller mud rush (*Juncus gerardii*). The sea rush is a perennial, tufts of shoots rising from the creeping root system. The stems are rigid, tough and pointed and can exceed a metre in height. The leaves are not as long as the stems but also end in points, and the pale flowers appear in lateral clusters protected by a long pointed bract, usually from July to September. The leaves of the mud rush are narrower and the whole plant is only about half a metre in height. The flowers appear at the same time as those of the sea rush but are carried in loose panicles at the end of the stems. Either of these rushes creates sufficient shade to kill off some vegetation, and the open soil is now more typical of the early zones. The odd slant of light will now allow the reappearance of algae and glassworts. To all intents and purposes the land has now been reclaimed from the sea and gradually typical terrestrial species enter the system. Farmland or even woodland come next in the logical line of succession, and our imaginary walk is at an end.

Pans and Drainage Channels

The saltings are not, as this account so far might indicate, level swards of vegetation but are pockmarked by depressions called pans and sliced by channels. The surface of a saltmarsh is never level, and water fills the lowest areas first, so that hummocks build up. If a group of hummocks join together to surround a lower area a depression is formed and water is not able to flow out when the tide ebbs; it may be able to percolate away or it may have to remain until the next tide. Should the pan be high up on the marsh it may only be reached by spring tides, and when hot weather coincides with neap tides the salinity may increase dramatically by evaporation. The pans may coalesce into channels which are eroded deeper and deeper by a combination of wind and spring tides. It is in this region that the saltmarsh plant sea purslane (*Halimione portulacoides*) comes into its own. It thrives on the well-drained banks and binds them firmly while the sea gradually deepens the channel between them. In flower from June to October, this shrub-like perennial grows from a tough, woody rootstock; the stems branch frequently and can reach over half a metre in length. It is particularly common along the east coast, where it dominates vast areas of creek, and it is also found in quantity along the south and south-west coast. It begins to thin out towards the north, and beyond the Duddon estuary it never assumes complete dominance of a large area of marsh.

Birds of the Saltmarsh Channels
To many wading birds these drainage channels provide excellent protection from wind and wather and allow them to feed in peace. Here

76

(*a*)

(*b*)

(*a*) *Redshank, with wing bar and* (*b*) *greenshank*

we may find the uncommon greenshank, the very uncommon spotted redshank and the very common redshank which so typifies the saltmarsh avifauna: not for nothing is this nervous bird called the warden of the marsh.

The greenshank (*Tringa nebularia*) is a taller, lighter-coloured bird than the redshank and its long green legs make it look large, although it measures only 30cm (1ft) in length. The slightly upturned bill is also typical and ideal for sweeping with a side-to-side movement through the shallows. On occasions the bird stands still for a moment and then rushes forwards with neck extended and bill submerged. When disturbed the greenshank's flight is twisting and erratic. The 'tew-tew-tew' call is lower-pitched than the redshank's, and a further difference is that an airborne greenshank has no white coloration on the wings. Only about 700 pairs of greenshanks breed in Britain and even these are confined to Scotland (mainly in the north and west), but many others pass through on passage to their northerly breeding grounds and they are now overwintering in increasing numbers. It is then that greenshanks find Britain's saltmarshes very much to their liking, providing both shelter and food, which includes crustaceans, worms, molluscs and small fish, but rarely any vegetation.

This diet is shared by the spotted redshank (*Tringa erythropus*), but the bills of the two species are so different that each has its own ecological niche and competition is avoided. In summertime the black, white-spotted plumage of the spotted redshank is unmistakable. In Britain, however, there are no breeding records and the winter plumage could be confused with that of the common redshank (*Tringa totanus*); but generally speaking the spotted redshank is a greyer bird with relatively longer legs and bill, and again there is no white to be seen on the wing during flight. In the common redshank, a broad white patch on the hind border of the wing is the bird's most prominent feature when in flight.

Any beginner in birdwatching who wishes to learn to identify waders has to pay particular attention to wing patterns and also to calls. The light note of the spotted redshank is a disyllabic 'tcheweet'; the common redshank utters either a single 'tuu' or a triple 'tu-hu-hu'. The spotted redshank breeds in Northern Europe and Siberia and winters in the Mediterranean and South Africa. Britain, being between the two, is the perfect resting-point for a passage migrant, and records are most frequent between July and mid-October; but as with the greenshank, an increasing number of birds are wintering here. The majority of records are coastal, the area between Lincolnshire and Hampshire being particularly favoured.

The redshank has something of a chequered history in Britain. Its numbers fell sharply at the beginning of the nineteenth century due to huge east coast drainage schemes which took place at this time. From then until the early 1840s the distribution seems to have been confined to the counties washed by the North Sea, beginning with the Orkneys and ending at Kent. From about 1865 the bird gradually spread to the west and south-west and this trend continued until 1940, since when there has been little significant change. One surprising feature is that until 1980 the common redshank had not been proved to breed in Cornwall, although a flock of about 300 birds always winters on the Camel estuary.

The British breeding population is in the order of 50,000 pairs, but they are scarce in the Outer Hebrides, Isle of Man and Ireland. The breeding areas are often occupied as early as mid-February. The nest is made on the ground, and the average clutch is four eggs, of a buff ground-colour spotted and blotched with purply-brown. The female lines the nest with dry grass but the incubation period of twenty-two to twenty-four days is shared by the two sexes. William Yarrell completed his monumental *British Birds* in 1843, and in it noted that:

> The redshank frequently breeds in small communities, and a score of nests may be found in a pasture or marsh of a few acres. The nest is well described by Col W. V. Legge, who says that it is concealed in the centre of a green tuft of grass, the blades of which are carefully bent over the top, and the openings, by which the bird enters and leaves the nest being closed up on her leaving it, only a few tracks in the surrounding herbage betraying its existence.

The breeding range is abandoned as soon as the young can fly. Some of these resident birds, which belong to our own sub-species *Tringa totanus britannica*, remain with us for the winter, being able to survive well because of their varied diet: it includes insects, molluscs and crustaceans and also vegetable matter such as leaves and energy-rich seeds and fruits. Some British breeders do migrate for the winter, travelling both to Ireland and the Continent, but they are replaced by even larger numbers of two other sub-species, *Tringa totanus robusta* (breeding in Iceland and the Faeroes) and *Tringa totanus totanus* (breeding from Scandinavia through Europe and even into Asia, which arrive via Northern Europe. Only in the breeding season, when it is paler than the other two, can the British race be distinguished from the other two sub-species without detailed dissection: I sometimes wonder why ornithologists trouble to separate them.

One of my greatest delights is to creep slowly through the cloying mud of a saltmarsh drainage channel to watch the waders, and I marvel at the guile of the wary redshanks which often swim across the creek rather than fly and thus give their position away. Once they do decide they must fly, however, they call so loudly that the whole marsh is alert: 'the warden of the marsh' has done its job once more.

Saltmarshes demonstrate the victory of vegetation over unstable, moving mud, taming it by root and stem. Nature does not always win the battle against inanimate matter but she never stops trying. Nowhere is this battle more obvious than when she challenges the relentless grinding tide turning the stones and pebbles that make up our shingle benches. Even here, as the next chapter will show, some remarkable success stories can be told.

4
Shingle Beaches

Naturalists tend to look at shingle beaches as the poor relations of our seaside habitats, but it must be accepted that a high percentage of our coastline has a shingle base and therefore deserves some attention. Shingle has been formed from rocks which have been battered free from their softer matrix, worn smooth and rounded into large stones, then pebbles and finally shingle. These pebbles are 'herded' along the coast by longshore currents and when a suitable flat surface becomes available they are pushed ashore, to form a beach. Such pebbly beaches tend to be very unstable and therefore unsuitable for plant growth. In addition to a moving substratum there is very little humus (the decaying remains of dead plants and animals on which plants depend) and this means little or no minerals for the roots of pioneering plants to absorb. Fresh water, surprisingly, is not a problem, because a sort of 'internal dew' seems to form within the shingle. On summer days the sun's heat drives the warmed air from between the stones and the threatened vacuum is prevented by cooler air being drawn in from above. This condenses on the warm stones and thus shingle plants are much better off for water than those of the saltmarshes.

Shingle beaches fall into four basic types: fringing shingle, shingle spits, shingle bars and apposition shingle beaches. On a fringing beach a ridge of pebbles is formed parallel to the sea, and plants can make use of the shelter which this provides and begin to stabilise the difficult substratum. A spit forms when the line of the coast abruptly turns inland, while the current carries on its original course so that it no longer follows the shore. The transported pebbles accumulate along the whole line of the current to form a bank or causeway which can in extreme cases be several miles in length; it remains attached to the land at the point where the coastline turns inwards. Many spits curve gently and since they are wider at their extremity they often hook in towards the land, since this side does not face erosion from the sea. Good examples of shingle spits are seen at Blakeney in Norfolk, Spurn Head in Yorkshire, Northam pebble ridge in Devon, Aldeburgh in Suffolk and Hurst Castle in Hampshire.

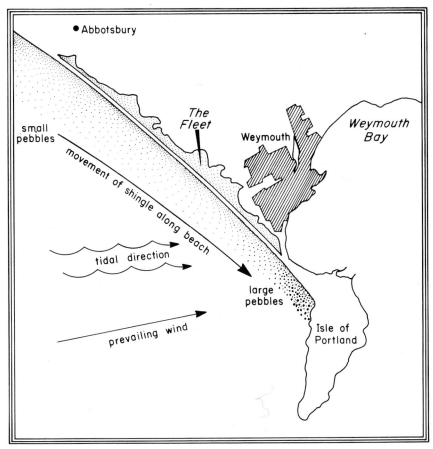

Chesil Beach, Dorset. The larger pebbles are swept down the beach leaving the smaller pebbles to form shingle beds at the Abbotsbury end

A shingle bar results if the hook turns so far that it joins up once more with the land, thus leaving a lagoon in the centre. This has happened to produce the Looe Bar in Cornwall and Dorset's Chesil Beach which is some 16km (10 miles) long and has enclosed an impressive lagoon known as the Fleet.

An apposition shingle beach builds up as new shingle is deposited on the side of an old beach, being rolled up against it until an abnormally high tide, plus the extra lift afforded by a storm-force wind, pushes it above normal tidal limits. Eventually a number of parallel ridges are formed and these are often extensive; Dungeness in Kent is the best known, others almost as impressive in their dimensions include Orford Ness on the Aldeburgh bank and Langney Point between Pevensey and Eastbourne. The great difference between apposition beaches and the

81

The low rocky coast at Axmouth, Lyme Regis shows the problems faced by plants trying to establish themselves on shingle (P. Wakely/Nature Conservancy Council)

other three types is that they are not mobile. Spits or bars, because of the constant battering they receive from the waves, move landwards; apposition beaches, apart from the outermost ridge, are sheltered from the waves, and their shingle is much more stable. Even here, however, the zonation which is so much a feature of saltmarsh vegetation is not obvious, although some workers, such as Petch in the 1930s and since then Chapman in the 1970s, suggest there are five areas on a typical shingle beach. Initially there is an area next to the sea so unstable that no plants will grow at all and this is followed by an area populated by summer-flowering annuals that take advantage of the relatively stable conditions between the high equinoctial tides of the spring and autumn. Some areas of beach, which constitute the third zone, remain stable for three or four years, and here poa (*Catapodium marinum*) and biting or yellow stonecrop (*Sedum acre*) may form a temporary mat of vegetation. The fourth zone is really a stable shingle beach and while the vegetation is never lush it can at times be quite impressive, including shrubby seablite, sea campion, yellow horned poppy, herb robert, sea kale and oyster plant (sea lungwort or northern shore weed). Should these plants succeed in stabilising the beach completely then a fifth zone may develop dominated by red fescue and oat-grass; this leads naturally into a heath-type vegetation and then the land is relatively safe from inundation from the sea.

Seablite, Sea Campion and Horned Poppy
Many of the early colonists are very interesting, not least the tough shrubby seablite (*Suaeda fruticosa*), a plant which is more at home in the warmer climate of the Mediterranean. In Britain it is decidedly local, but growing often in great abundance in places such as Dorset's Chesil Beach and the north coast of Norfolk from Weybourne to Hunstanton. Sea walls and shingle on the Essex marshes, Poole Harbour and areas near Cardiff also have substantial growths of this branching woody shrub which reaches a height of about a metre on stable shingle; it is well supplied with succulent bright green leaves, often tinged with purple or even crimson. To all intents and purposes the plant is evergreen, since its leaves from one year are not shed until the next crop are already bursting from bud. The small green flowers appear in August, growing from the axils of the leaves. By the end of November the fruits (each of which contains a small glossy black seed) are ripe, and it seems that about once in four years a massive crop is produced. Shrubby seablite does not seem to flourish in dull wet autumns and it may well be this which limits its distribution.

It is a very important plant in stabilising shingle and has been cultivated for this reason. When the beach is still mobile and buries the

Shrubby seablite

plant from time to time, this only serves to stimulate its growth, and eventually the mobility of the pebbles is slowed and finally halted altogether. Another characteristic is that it grows quickly, and once stabilised, parts of the rhizome system break down into a rich humus which allows other species to find sufficient nourishment to carry on the colonisation.

Sea campion (*Silene maritima*) is a common plant around the coast, and was at one time thought to be a variety of the bladder campion (*Silene vulgaris*). Work done by Marsden-Jones and Turril, however, suggests that the sea campion in Britain survived the Ice Ages but the bladder campion recolonised our islands after the ice had receded. Nevertheless the occasional hybrid between the two does occur. Sea campion is a perennial plant with a tough branched rootstock from which a cushion of leaves, and also shoots, spring in profusion. This rosette arrangement resists wind and sea. As with seablite, burial beneath shingle seems to stimulate growth; sea campion reacts more slowly, but given time it can have a great stabilising influence on a beach. From the thick, fleshy leaves spring the single white flowers, from April to October. The stem can reach a length of 25cm (10in), and the petals are notched and larger than those of the bladder campion. The seeds are dispersed when the wind shakes their perforated capsule just as we shake a pepper pot.

The yellow horned poppy (*Glaucium flavum*) also occurs around our coastline, but its distribution is uneven. Its beauty is often underrated, the red poppy of the cornfields being far better known – as the poet Robert Bridges knew:

> A poppy grows upon the shore,
> Bursts her twin cup in summer late:
> Her leaves are glaucous green and hoar,
> Her petals yellow, delicate.
>
> Oft to her cousins turns her thought
> In wonder if they care that she
> Is fed with spray for dew, and caught
> By every gale that sweeps the sea.
>
> She has no lovers like the red,
> That dances with the noble corn:
> Her blossoms on the waves are shed,
> Where she stands shivering and forlorn.

Many yellow poppies shiver on Chesil Beach, and are characteristic of other shingle beaches, but in parts of Scotland the plant is quite rare. Like sea campion it arises from a woody rootstock and can be either

Frosted orache growing on a shingle and pebble beach (Author)

84

perennial or biennial. It has a deep vertical taproot which ensures a supply of fresh dew water from amongst the pebbles. It can also survive being covered by a high tide by having an extensive covering of water-resistant hairs. Again a rosette of leaves proves to be an ideal arrangement for an exposed habitat, the flowering stem grows from the centre of this mat and during the summer may reach a metre in length. The beautiful yellow flowers which so impressed Robert Bridges can be as much as 8cm (over 3in) across and from these the long thin pods containing the seeds are produced.

The plant produces an orange-coloured sap which smells unpleasant but was used at one time in the treatment of bruises. The plant was locally known as 'bruise root' or 'bruise wort', and also as 'squat' or 'squatmore', the word squat being Old English for bruise. The treatment was to rub the juice on to the bruise and not to take it by mouth as an interesting record in the Royal Society's *Philosophical Transactions* shows:

> A certain person made a pye of the roots of this plant, supposing them to be the roots of the Eryngo [sea holly, see Chapter 5] of which he had before eaten pyes which were very pleasant, and eating it while it was hot, became delirious, and having voided a stool in a white chamber pot, fancied it to be gold, breaking the pot in pieces, and desiring what he imagined was gold might be preserved as such. Also his man and maid servant eating of the same pye, fancied of what they saw to be gold.

Cranesbills, Sea Kale and Oyster Plant

The yellow horned poppy is not the only shingle-based plant with a rather unpleasant smell, for herb robert, that tough little 'stinker' as it was called in the old days, grows there as it does almost everywhere else. It is an annual plant, usually starting to flower in April but still to be found in bloom well into autumn. I once found herb-robert flowers on a shingle beach at Aldingham, Cumbria on 12 November. It can grow to a height of 60cm (2ft) in ideal conditions, but on shingle it is prostrate and rather stunted. The hairy stems are much branched and often bright red. The leaves are compound, divided into five segments each of which is then further divided. The flowers are neatly arranged, as in the rest of the cranesbill family; five sepals make up the calyx, five pink petals the corolla and within these are ten stamens. The cranesbill family gets its name from the long beak-shaped fruits. The red colour of the stems earned herb robert a place in the herbalists' repertoire, despite what Gerard described as 'its most loathsome stinking smell', and judging by the number of its vernacular names – Grigson listed 107 – it was well known to our ancestors, although its reputation was not good. According to the old doctrine of signatures, the red of the plant, like the red breast of a robin, meant that the plant was associated with that

wicked old house-goblin Robin Goodfellow; should any of his poss-
essions be taken into a human dwelling then literally all hell was likely
to be let loose. This is reflected in the vernacular names of felonwort,
headache, robin redbreast and, more forcibly, 'death come quickly'. It
was also supposed to have sexual significance, as indicated by other
names including kiss-me-quick, hedge lovers and jack flower.

On the south and west coasts of Britain herb robert is sometimes
joined by another member of the *Geraniaceae* family, the purple
cranesbill (*Geranium pupureum*). This smells less, is hairier, has duller
flowers and yellow not red, anthers. Favoured sites for purple cranesbill
include Chesil Beach and the shingle shores of Sussex.

Two other plants which are decidedly local in their distribution are
the sea kale and the oyster plant. Sea kale (*Crambe maritima*, is a large
strong plant and where it occurs, at Pevensey, Calshot and Cemlyn, for
example, it exerts an important stabilising influence. Once a highly
prized vegetable, the plant has been reduced by collection rather than
being limited in original distribution. Unlike shrubby seablite, sea kale
does not occur in the Mediterranean. William Curtis (1746–99) wrote a
pamphlet called *Directions for the culture of the Crambe maritima or sea
kale, for the use of the table.* The cabbage-like leaves are not so pleasant as
the blanched shoots, which were known as 'sickel' or 'sickels' and served
fried in breadcrumbs and doused with lemon juice, or with toast and
lashings of butter. The sickels can also be boiled and eaten like
asparagus. The large white flowers which appear from June to August
can measure as much as 1.5cm across (just over $\frac{1}{2}$in) and grow in
crowded showy clusters; the resultant seed pods are egg-shaped.

The oyster plant or sea lungwort, often called northern shoreweed
(*Mertensia maritima*), is found in America, Asia, Europe and parts of
Britain – occasionally in Scotland, in a few areas of northern England,
including Roanhead in Cumbria and Blakeney in Norfolk, and also in
Anglesey. The thick, fleshy, spotted leaves have a faint taste of oysters,
hence the most common vernacular name; but through the doctrine of
signatures it was thought useful for treating respiratory disorders, and
earned the alternative name of lungwort. The tiny 0.6cm ($\frac{1}{4}$in) flowers,
at the ends of the branches from May to August, are purplish-pink at
first, changing to a delicate blue, possibly after pollination.

Birds of Shingle Beaches
Some of the plants discussed reach the beach when their seeds are
carried on the waves of the sea, but birds bring many more, stuck to
their feet or voided in their droppings. Shingle beaches are never
attractive areas for feeding birds, but in some areas stands of curled
dock (*Rumex crispus* var *maritima*) provide rich food for autumnal
migrating birds, including yellowhammers. Greenfinches may be seen

feeding on the seeds of carline thistle and thrift, which occasionally succeed in getting a roothold in some of the more stable areas.

Birds such as pied wagtails, wheatears and ringed plover search along the strandline and beneath pebbles in search of food. Although invertebrates are not as common as in estuaries or on sandy shores, there are a number of worms, including the lugworm (*Arenicola marina*), and some crustaceans, including sandhoppers (*Talitrus saltator*), shore skippers (*Orchestia gammarella*) and a number of species of isopods otherwise known as sea slaters. Like the sandhoppers the slaters, woodlouse-type creatures, have almost severed their dependence upon the sea and do not even require it to breed; the female carries her young about with her in a brood pouch until they are able to look after themselves. All isopods are nocturnal and will not venture forth if bright moonlight, leave alone sunlight, illuminates the beach. There are about twenty species. The gribble (*Limnoria lignorum*) may be found on wood washed up on to shingle beaches: the holes it bores in the timber will be seen. Beneath debris and pebbles will be found the common sea slater (*Ligia oceanica*). This flat greenish-brown segmented animal, up to 2.5cm (1in) in length, makes a tasty meal for the ringed plover, which is so adept at turning over the pebbles. If ever a species could be considered to be perfectly adapted to life on this type of beach it must surely be this bird; in my home county of Cumbria and in the counties of Norfolk and Sussex, it is known as the stone runner.

The ringed plover (*Charadrius hiaticula*) is a robust little bird, almost 20cm (8in) long with a prominent black collar with bold black and white markings on the side and front of the head. A well-marked, narrow white wing bar at once distinguishes it from the little ringed plover (*Charadrius dubius*), which also has a yellow ring around the eye and in any case is more of an inland breeder, although not exclusively so. Since its first breeding in 1938 the little ringed plover has increased very rapidly, due to its ability to use derelict areas as breeding sites. I was once, back in 1973, watching ringed plover displaying on an old ironworks on the Duddon estuary, when my attention was drawn to a pair of what turned out to be mating little ringed plover. This ironworks has been demolished since the 1920s and runs into a shingle beach, so here I observed, possibly for the first time in Britain, the two similar species breeding on natural and 'artificial' shingle within 50m (150yd) of each other.

While the population of little ringed plover is rising, that of the common ringed plover is showing serious signs of decline, though still in the order of 7,000 pairs. It has been pointed out (Sharrock, 1976) that many of the clutches of eggs laid on shingle beaches never hatch. This is entirely due to disturbance by human activities. The four cryptically coloured eggs are almost impossible to see among the pebbles, and the

Eggs of the ringed plover on shingle (Author)

beach anglers and casual holidaymakers who notice the birds flying anxiously about don't know enough about natural history to realise that a nest is there. Should the day be cold and wet (or should the anglers be operating at night), the eggs chill and the embryos perish; on a hot summer day, unturned eggs, deprived of the parents' shelter, literally fry in the heat of the sun. The oyster-catcher (*Haematopus ostralegus*) also has these problems but is more adaptable in its choice of nest site and is therefore coping with the pressures. The little tern (*Sterna albifrons*) does not cope at all, and badly needs habitat protection, a factor well appreciated by the RSPB, who are trying to give that on their coastal reserves.

The terns in general find shingle beaches ideal nesting sites. Foulney and Walney in Cumbria, as well as Dungeness in Kent, are among many reserves in which they are now guaranteed protection. We need more such reserves, for although shingle, as we have seen, is not the richest natural habitat, the pebbles can often be important in helping to trap sand. From this, at Blakeney and Scolt Head in Norfolk for example, impressive sand dunes have evolved from a shingle base.

5
Sand Dunes

The most profitable way of making a study of sand dunes is to stroll out to the strandline of a sandy shore and turn your back on the sea, as you might do when exploring the zones of a saltmarsh. If you make the visit on a day of high wind and spring tide, you will appreciate how tough it must be for a plant trying to establish itself among this driving sand. In contrast it is easy to see how any obstruction that has established a hold can trap sand and thus originate a small dune. Any consideration of the flora and fauna of sand dunes must recognise a series of well-defined areas, beginning with the driftline itself, moving to the mobile dunes at an early stage of formation, and then to the stable or fixed dunes which eventually develop into woodland or heathland. Finally we must note the wet patches (or slacks) between the dunes, which have their own fascinating communities.

The Driftline

By its very nature the driftline must be unstable, but – especially during a warm calm summer – it can often be a good hunting ground for botanists on the lookout for rare species such as oyster plant, sea kale and sea radish.

Sea radish (*Raphanus maritimus*) is usually described as a biennial plant but it is also a perennial: there may be two slightly different types, and I look forward to some scientifically minded university student trying to separate biennial from perennial type by selective breeding. Who knows – we might be dealing with sub-species. As every scientist knows, it is easy to formulate a question, decidedly more difficult to answer it. When sea radish grows on the driftline it tends to be small and stunted; further inland, in the shelter of the dune system, it grows considerably taller. Some years ago a seed or two must have been unwittingly transported to my garden some 90 miles inland in a small bucket of sand and shells taken home for my young son to play with. From this humble beginning a flourishing population of perennial sea radish developed and some individuals reached heights of over a metre.

Sea rocket on the driftline (Author)

The colour of the flowers varies from white to pale yellow and, like all members of the crucifer family, they have four petals in the form of a cross. It is not the flowers which fascinate me, however, but the pod-like fruits which are segmented, each segment terminating in a beak-like structure that contains a single seed which can float; this is the reason why sea radish is a member of the driftline community.

So is another crucifer, the sea rocket, as well as sea sandwort, shore orache, sea campion, the knot grasses and the once very useful prickly saltwort (*Salsola kali*). This straggling humble annual fixes loose sand, and can sometimes originate a mini-dune. A succulent, it can absorb

91

Prickly saltwort (Author)

large volumes of salt, and at one time was collected and burned, with glasswort, to produce the soda used in the manufacture of glass and soap. It has proved well able to survive periodic immersion in sea water, the stems and leaves being liberally covered by water-repellent hairs. For the flowers, which occur from July to October, look in the leaf axils, where the single green, sometimes pink, structures with pale yellow anthers can be found by the keen-sighted.

All these pioneer plants must be halophytes or at least have some tolerance of salt; but the influence of the tide is not always detrimental. It delivers to the strandline a regular supply of rotting vegetation and hence there are often more minerals available here than in the sheltered dunelands.

The strandline is also attractive to some insects, especially the predatory ground beetle (*Pogonus chalceus*), black but with a purplish sheen on its back in sunlight. This creature is only about half a centimetre long (one-fifth of an inch), about half the size of the seaweed-eating kelp fly (*Suillia ustulata*). Although this creature does not bite it often rises in swarms around the beach and annoys the holidaymaker. It is a rather hairy beast, silvery-grey in colour, and has translucent wings with spines on the front margins. Darting swiftly about, especially during the nuptial flight, kelp flies lay eggs in rotting seaweed; from these hatch the legless larvae, which form a juicy meal for many a predator, including the ground beetle and such birds as pied wagtail and stonechat. Indeed feeding on the strandline may have enabled the stonechat to remain a resident in Britain rather than migrate, as is the custom of its insect-eating relative the whinchat. Both species take caterpillars and other invertebrates during the summer and when the winter freezes these into concealed hibernation the whinchat must head south. The stonechat, however, is happy to take a short winter break at the seaside, where the high salt content prevents the strandline from freezing and the rotting vegetation produces a little heat which keeps the invertebrates in it alive and active. This useful food supply is also tapped by a rare winter visitor, the snow bunting, as well as a common summer visitor, the wheatear.

Early Dunes

When sand drives across an open beach it may be halted by shingle, by one of the strandline plants, or more than likely by one of three grasses, the sea couch grass (*Agropyron junceiforme*), sea lyme grass (*Elymus arenarius*) and the well-known marram (*Ammophila arenaria*). The former often plays the part of chief scout, preparing the ground for the more vigorous-looking marram which is unable to stand immersion in sea water, as couch grass can. In the early stages the sand is very mobile but the extensive creeping rhizomes eventually bind it, and gradually the dune increases in height. It is at this point that the usefulness of couch grass is at an end because it does not have the power to grow its way out when buried by blown sand. Nor has sea lyme grass, which can only produce mini-dunes. Marram, on the other hand, once free of salt spray, thrives on being buried by a moderate wind responding with vigorous growth at a staggering speed. The plant really gets a grip on the crests of the young dunes and then spreads its rhizomes through it, binding it tight. High winds punch holes into the dunes, however, forming what are technically called 'blow-outs'. In time even these wounds will be healed.

Obviously the side of the dune facing the sea will be the least stable and any other plants typical of early dunes will most likely be found on the leeward side. Many factors, however, contribute to making dunes a most hostile environment for seedlings, even in sheltered spots. There is, for example lots and lots of sand, but few plants, and this means far less humus than is found on the strandline. Add to this the quick-draining properties of sand and it can be readily appreciated that only deep roots of established plants will have reliable water supplies and

93

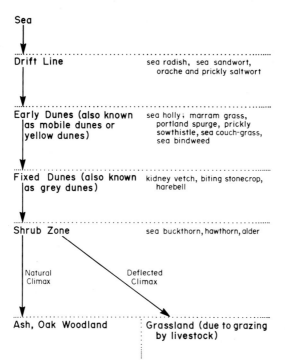

Sea
↓
....
Drift Line   sea radish, sea sandwort,
                                    orache and prickly saltwort
↓
....
Early Dunes (also known   sea holly; marram grass,
as mobile dunes or   portland spurge, prickly
yellow dunes)   sowthistle, sea couch-grass,
                           sea bindweed
↓
....
Fixed Dunes (also known kidney vetch, biting stonecrop,
as grey dunes)   harebell
↓
....
Shrub Zone   sea buckthorn, hawthorn, alder

Natural   Deflected
Climax   Climax
↓
....
Ash, Oak Woodland   Grassland (due to grazing
                             by livestock)

Possible plant succession in a sand dune

newcomers will have a job to survive the early stages of growth. There is evidence to suggest that some 'internal dew' may be produced between the tiny particles of sand, much as dew is formed between pebbles on a shingle beach (see Chapter 4). Another problem for the delicate seedling is the great fluctuation in temperature which can occur on open sand dunes.

Gradually a few plants succeed in rooting and then comes an accelerating build-up, of both species and populations. Traditional coastal species such as sea holly, sea bindweed, portland spurge and sun spurge are now joined by inland plants such as yellow stonecrop, groundsel, ragwort, carline thistle and many others. Gradually these plants stabilise the habitat sufficiently to allow mosses with their shallow rhizoids (equivalent to the roots of the higher plants) to grow on the surface. Obviously a delicate plant like a moss cannot survive here until there are stronger plants to give it some protection. *Tortula ruraliformis* is a common moss on sand dunes, and indeed is restricted to this habitat, and it is often accompanied by *Camptothecium lutescens*, *Bryum argenteum*, *Bryum capillare* and *Bryum pendulum*. Mosses do

Sowthistle – a plant which thrives on developing sand dunes (Author)

95

need more water than flowering plants, but many have xerophytic devices (water-retaining structures), including infolded leaves and rolled margins, to assist their survival during the dry periods of summer.

Into these semi-fixed dunes come two groups of plants, the so-called winter annuals and the perennials. The winter annuals are shallow-rooted and pass through their life cycle during winter and spring, before the advent of the summer droughts. Included in the long list are thyme-leaved sandwort, early forget-me-not, corn salad, sand chickweed and sand catstail. Perennials regularly found on dune systems at this stage in their development include white clover, silverweed, yellow or lady's bedstraw, yellow rattle, bird's-foot trefoil and mouse-eared hawkweed (*Hieracium pilosella*). These and other species combine to produce a stable dune, which is then said to be fixed.

Amongst the many interesting and at one time useful plants found here are silverweed and sea holly.

Silverweed (*Potentilla anserina*)

Potentilla means 'the little powerful one', an apt description since the plant was a vital food for the poor before the introduction of the potato and also as a substitute when the new 'foreign' crop failed. The roots were eaten raw, roasted or boiled, or ground into meal which could later be mixed with water and baked into flat unleavened 'bread'. They were used by herbalists in the treatment of ulcers, either in the mouth or caused by wounds, and as they delicately put it 'of the privy parts'. For those who walked many miles carrying heavy loads the leaves placed in the shoes were supposed to prevent blisters on the feet. The name 'silverweed' comes from the white hairs which cover the leaves, especially on the underside. The leaves of plants growing on the seashore seem to be hairier than those found in inland habitats, which must help in the retention of fresh water. Silverweed has a slender rootstock and the attractive flower has five shiny yellow petals. The dark red nectar is secreted from the base of the petals and ensures a regular stream of insect visitors. Should these fail to cross-pollinate a plant, then the act of closing its petals tightly during rain or at night may press the reproductive parts together so closely that the plant pollinates itself. Here is another example of nature hedging her bets.

Sea Holly

Like silverweed, sea holly (*Eryngium maritimum*) is aptly named since its leaves are prickly and very like those of the holly, although it is a member of the compositae (daisy) family and not even remotely related to the holly. The once common species is now thinly distributed around the coast, due to the fact that the roots were once dug up, soaked in

Sea holly growing amongst marram grass (Author)

sugar and orange-flower water and sold under the name of snow eringoes, a practice which only disappeared as the confectionery trade developed. Sea holly is another example of a xerophytic plant perfectly adapted, like true desert plants, for living in conditions of water shortage. Sand dunes are just as typical of parched inland areas in some parts of the world, the Sahara for example, as they are of coastal Britain. To conserve every precious drop of water, the leaves of sea holly are curled inwards, their spiny edges almost meeting at times, and the whole leaf is covered in a thick cuticle of waxy material. It is a perennial plant with very long creeping roots, doubtless of great importance as a survival factor in high winds. Like marram grass, though not quite as efficiently, if sea holly is buried by a sand drift it can accelerate its growth upwards until it surfaces once more. It may be prickly and a nuisance to picnickers, but when in full bloom during July and August its bluish flowers and leaves seem to sparkle clear and crisp in the sunlight, and adding interest and beauty to the dunes in the eyes of even the most casual visitor.

Fixed Dunes

Established dunes form an attractive feature of the coastline of many counties; in Wales they are called warrens, in Devon and Cornwall burrows, and in Norfolk meols. In Scotland the accepted word is links, while in the Western Isles of Scotland the machair, the typical pasture formed behind the dunes, has great appeal to nature-lovers.

Once the ground is stabilised, lichens are able to move in, but they cannot play any major role until the dune surface has reached a fairly mature stage. Lichens are a combination of two plants, a fungus which anchors both of them and a green alga which as a result of its photosynthetic efficiency provides enough food for both. Neither of the two organisms is able to live an independent existence; such a partnership is known as symbiosis (sharing life).

The most common lichens found on fixed dunes are species of *Peltigera* and *Cladonia*, they can occur in such numbers that the whole area looks grey. Yellow and white dunes are younger, their surface colour caused by chemical rather than biological factors. If iron salts are present there tend to be low levels of calcium carbonate and the dune takes on a yellowish appearance; if calcium carbonate, usually in the form of shell fragments, is plentiful then the dune is white.

At this stage marram grass seems to have outlived its usefulness and becomes less dominant; this can certainly not be due to any shading effect since it has no taller rivals here. It may be that there is some change in the chemical nature of the soil, or that some chemical produced by the new arrivals inhibits its growth. Whatever the reason, it slowly fades out of the picture. It is obvious from the very nature of sand dunes that lime-loving plants (the so-called calcicolous species) will thrive and, many of these such as kidney vetch or ladies' fingers, viper's bugloss, salad burnet, ploughman's spikenard, purging or fairy flax and the curious and poisonous henbane are of interest, particularly the latter species which has a long medical history; it grows in large stands on the dunes of Walney Island in particular.

Those who practised the science of signatures were not slow to notice that a branch of henbane (*Hyoscyamus niger*) complete with seeds looked like a human jaw complete with a set of molar teeth. It was therefore used, probably by the Greeks, as a cure for toothache and no doubt it worked, but it must have had a number of drastic side-effects. The stems and leaves contain a very powerful alkaloid poison, hyoscine, which acts as a brain sedative to calm down mentally excitable patients and as a cure for the horrors of sea-sickness. Overdoses can kill and henbane was the drug used by the infamous Dr Crippen to murder his

Massive dune system with active erosion and species-rich grassland, Dunnet links, Caithness (P. Wakely/Nature Conservancy Council)

Harebell on dunes (Author)

wife in 1910. It is an annual plant with an unpleasant smell. The leaves are large, viscid and hairy, the flowers yellowish-white with prominent purple veins.

Scarlet pimpernel is found frequently in this area which may well have been its original habitat: weeds like this and some other annuals such as forget-me-nots and lesser chickweed probably owe their present abundance to man's constant disturbance of ground. Before our activities many of them would have been quite rare and restricted to open habitats such as sand dunes.

Burnet and Forester Moths

Ragwort (*Senecio jacobaea*) also grows well in these situations, and at times can be almost the dominant plant – much to the benefit of a 'locally distributed' moth, the six-spot burnet (*Zygaena filipendulae*) as well as the cinnabar moth (*Callimorpha jacobaeae*). An interesting example of how nature balances her books is the close relationship between the relative fortunes of the cinnabar moth and ragwort. When

Cinnabar moth caterpillars feeding on ragwort (Author)

there are plenty of the bright black-and-yellow caterpillars they make such inroads into the plants that few seeds are set. Next year there are fewer plants for the larvae to eat and so their population drops and the following year the ragwort can recover its numbers. 'Local' distribution is the term used when the number of areas in which a plant or animal is found are limited, but when it does occur the populations can be very high. The six-spot burnet belongs to the family of Zygaenid moths

(*Zygaenidae*), which is made up of a great number of species, mainly tropical or sub-tropical. The number of European species diminishes the further north you go, and there are only about ten species in Britain today; all these are day-flying. Three are referred to as forester moths, the others as burnets. All the species tend to be colonial and this is certainly true of the six-spot, which often reaches almost plague proportions on some of our dune systems during July and August when the adults feed and copulate upon ragwort, thyme, bird's-foot trefoil and knapweed.

The wing length of the six-spot burnet can reach 2cm (0.8in), the ground colour being shiny black except for the six red spots arranged in pairs. These spots are usually distinct, but if they merge together then some confusion between this and other less common burnets may result. The caterpillar is greenish with black markings and some yellow spots, particularly around the openings to the spiracles (breathing holes). It feeds in the autumn, chiefly on trefoils such as kidney vetch, bird's-foot trefoil and white clover, and hibernates as a caterpillar, completing its growth during the spring. The cocoon is a conspicuous yellow structure strung along a strand of dead grass, very often marram. Then there are the numerous cinnabar-moth caterpillars feeding on the ragwort, and the dune vegetation is attacked by many other butterfly and moth larvae, including those of grayling, common blue and meadow brown. Insects are plentiful in the dunes, but so are birds, which exert some semblance of control over their numbers.

Sand and Spider Wasps

Predators of insects also come from within their own ranks; none is more formidable than the red-banded sand wasp (*Ammophila sabulosa*). It was the eminent nineteenth-century French naturalist, Fabre, who first described how female sand wasps paralyse caterpillars with their sting, and then carry off the living but immobilised prey to a nest. The wasp's eggs are then laid in the caterpillar's body, and when the grubs hatch they eat the unfortunate creature alive. The pupae remain dormant for long periods and it is only in July and August that the adult wasp is about. It can be recognised by its very narrow 'waist' with the wide red band that gives it its name. It is about 2.5cm long (1in) and can often be seen resting, or maybe seeking prey, on the leaves of sea holly. Fabre is not the only well-known naturalist to have studied its habits, Niko Tinbergen having done some interesting experiments on the behaviour of sand wasps in the 1930s, long before he made his name with his studies of gulls. Tinbergen found that sand wasps have a well-developed homing instinct, the females being well able to find their own burrows provided nothing happens to disturb the natural features of their habitat.

Sand lizards, a rare and declining species (Dr Ian F. Spellerberg)

Another predator of the dunes is the spider wasp (*Pompilius cinerens*), which pushes its paralysing sting into spiders, plentiful enough during the summer, including the wolf spider, crab spider and money spider.

The Sand Lizard

Any insect is under threat in sand hills haunted by lizards. Britain has three surviving species: the slow-worm, which we have already met in Chapter 1, the fairly widespread common lizard (*Lacerta vivipara*) and the rare sand lizard (*Lacerta agilis*), whose distribution is now sadly restricted, mainly because of loss of habitat; but it may still be found on the heaths and dunes of Dorset, Hampshire and the Isle of Wight. Despite statements to the contrary, both common and sand lizard occur in sand dunes: they must be distinguished on more scientific evidence than habitat. The common lizard's specific name, *vivipara*, of course indicates that it gives birth to live young; the sand lizard, in contrast, lays eggs. This difference obviously does not help you to identify the little lizard that slips away on the sand dune, but if you can see its underparts you may get a clue: the sand lizard often has a green abdomen, especially the males in spring. Positive identification of the female sand lizard is more of a problem, though she too may have some green colour on her belly. If anything, the sand lizard is larger than the common lizard, but there is not much in it: the common lizard male averages about 17cm (6¾in), the female 17.8cm (7in), whereas the male sand lizard averages 19.3cm ($7\frac{5}{8}$in), the female 18.5cm ($7\frac{3}{8}$in).

During May and June the sand lizard lays about ten eggs, oval and about 8cm ($\frac{1}{2}$in) in diameter. The female digs a hole in the sand for them, and they can take anything from seven to twelve weeks to hatch, depending on temperature. The young look like small versions of the adults. Great efforts must now be made to save this, one of Britain's rarest animals. If one of our birds had declined so rapidly during this century there would have been an outcry, yet it is just as important to protect the sand lizard – now! It has been given special protection in the Wildlife and Countryside Act but it needs more than conservation – it needs positive help. An increasing number of dune systems are being designated as nature reserves and this should certainly help. In the past the natural succession has been interfered with; once a stable heathland developed behind the shelter of the dunes, it was 'planted' with bungalows or caravans, or developed into golf courses. If left alone that heathland would gradually develop into grassland or even woodland. In some parts of Britain deliberate afforestation has been attempted in an effort to give nature a hand. The best example here is perhaps the Culbin sands on the Moray Firth.

Dune Shrubs

A stable dune will gradually become dominated by shrubs such as dog rose, burnet rose, sea buckthorn, hazel, elder, hawthorn, blackthorn, honeysuckle, brambles and even privet. Of all the dune shrub species listed here, only the sea buckthorn and the burnet rose are to be regarded as seaside plants occasionally found inland, rather than the reverse.

Along stretches of the east coast, sea buckthorn (*Hippophae rhamnoides*) can become dominant and in a few areas on the west coast, Ainsdale for instance, it has been planted as a dune binder. It is possibly only native from Yorkshire to Sussex. It is certainly important at Spurn Head, where it also gives cover and food to a host of migrant birds, many rarities being recorded; this is reflected in the number of bird-watchers there, armed with batteries of optical aids. Although the shrub can reach a height of over 4 metres, it is generally much more compact. The long lance-like leaves are greenish-grey on the upper surface, but the under-surface is quite scaly, some being rusty, others silvery-white. The plant is dioecious, which means that there are male and female trees; only the female trees bear the attractive berries, which fieldfares and redwings seek each autumn, as do waxwings on their occasional eruptions into Britain from Northern Europe. The insignificant green flowers are found from May until early August. The berries are seen at their best in November, especially in the early sunlight after a night of frost.

104

The burnet rose (*Rosa spinosissima*) grows thick on some of our dunes. It is among my favourite plants, not only because of its delightful flowers and sturdy, attractive habit, but because it gave me my first financial 'independence', at the age of seven. During the 1939–45 war, country children could earn 3d (just over 1p) a pound for collecting the fruits of the dog rose and field rose. We all entered the world of high finance and then I found my secret weapon – the hips of the burnet rose were bringing not 3d but 4d a pound. The plant, covered with shining purplish hips, was there on my Cumbrian sand hills, and I well remember the thrill of learning the four-times table! The fruits went to a factory to be made into rose-hip syrup, a rich source of vitamin C when ships were too busy with wartime activities to bring fresh fruit (my old granny even went back to eating scurvy-grass leaves).

The name burnet rose was given because the leaves resemble those of the salad burnet, but it is also, more appropriately, called the burrow rose; on the Pembroke dunes it is called St David's rose, and it is the emblem of the See of St David's, Britain's smallest diocese.

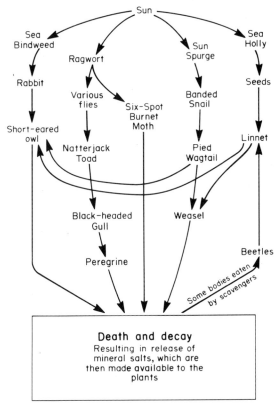

Simplified food web of a sand dune

Amongst this impressive mass of vegetation, ground- and shrub-nesting birds abound, including skylark, meadow pipit, yellowhammer, linnet and stonechat. Where patches of fresh water occur the reed bunting finds an ideal habitat, and represents a stage where land and sea birds merge happily. The various seagulls must be the most typical dune-nesting birds, but only three prefer this to other seaside habitats. Opposite is a summary of our six breeding gulls, so that they should be fairly easily identifiable. The herring gull, lesser black-backed gull, greater black-backed gull and black-headed gull are very much birds of the dunes. A large population of them can change a dune dominated by marram grass, as it is affected both by their physical tramplings and by the chemicals in their droppings. Winter annuals, especially chickweed, take advantage of the bare ground to establish themselves.

The Herring Gull

This gull is presenting problems for local health authorities. More than one seaside town has tried several methods of reducing the local population of herring gulls, which keep people awake at night and on the alert during the day if they are not to be unpleasantly 'white-washed'. Shooting birds is not a pleasant activity for visitors to witness, and in any case is impossible in a public place. Climbing on to roofs to remove large numbers of nests, which may then simply be constructed afresh, is hardly practicable and so they tried making a tape-recording of the birds' alarm call; this was then amplified and played at the birds to frighten them away. The alarm call may well work on a gull roost, but a gull in its breeding territory is a different proposition altogether: it simply treats the call as a threat, to be met by a suitable defence, and reacts by stretching upright to scream a reply. This raises the noise level, and the situation is worse than ever!

The species breeds in Iceland, the British Isles and north-western Europe as far as the Baltic. A great deal of work was done on it by Professor Niko Tinbergen, whose book *A Herring Gull's World* was published in 1953; a film called 'Signals for Survival' was made for BBC television in 1969, having been shot on Walney Island Nature Reserve near Barrow-in-Furness in Cumbria. Niko Tinbergen studied the natural history of the herring gull in detail, but concentrated in the main on its behaviour. Having over 40,000 nests to watch, he was not short of subjects. Gradually it became apparent that the herring gull has its own 'language'. It uses a 'keew' call when warning off a potential predator. This is usually followed by a determined attack, as many a visitor to a gullery in the breeding period will testify. When setting up a nesting territory, the herring gull stands with its head thrust out and utters a string of very loud 'keew-keew-keew' calls: this Tinbergen named 'the long call'. It is used as a challenge to any rival gull. Gulls are

Identification Clues for Adult Gulls

	SIZE	BEAK COLOUR	EYE COLOUR	PLUMAGE	LEG COLOUR	BRITISH BREEDING POPULATION (THOUSANDS OF PAIRS)
Black-headed gull	38cm (15in)	Red	Eyelids white	White, silver-grey back and wings. Head chocolate in summer, white in winter, with a few chocolate spots. Wings have black tips	Red	75
Herring gull	57cm (22in)	Yellow, hooked at tip. Red spot on bill	Yellow, with orange ring round	White back, wings silver-grey. Black wing-tips with white spots	Pink	360
Lesser black-backed gull	54cm (21in)	Yellow	Yellow	All white, but a dark back. Wings have white edges	Yellow	50
Common gull	41cm (16in)	Yellow-green	White or yellow	Similar to herring gull, but smaller	Yellow-green	12
Great black-backed gull	73cm (29in)	Yellow	Grey	Like a very large lesser black-backed gull, with blacker back	Pink	20
Kittiwake	40cm (16in)	Yellow-green	Orange ring around eye	White with silver-grey on back. Tail slightly forked. Black wing-tips	Black	470

amongst the most aggressive of birds but they have periods when they show great tenderness. A gentle 'mew' is used when the young are being attended to, and also a 'choking' call, uttered while pointing the head downwards, opening the bill and rhythmically jerking the body. A sound like 'huch-huch' is used during courtship when the male feeds the female on regurgitated food and also when either parent is feeding the young.

In addition to vocal signals, birds use visual signals. A careful look at the bill of an adult herring gull reveals a red spot on the lower mandible. The young will not take food until they see this red spot and their insistent pecking at it persuades the adult to regurgitate food. The diet of the adults is surprisingly diverse, which is a further reason for the success of the species. They will eat birds which are too young or too weak to defend themselves; they also eat eggs, especially those of their neighbours: a gullery in June, July and early August is a jungle where only the fittest survive. Eggs are bashed open and eaten, wandering and unwary chicks swallowed whole. Surveys carried out by the Royal Society for the Protection of Birds have shown that herring gulls sometimes eat peculiar objects, including putty; a toy rubber 'Dracula' bat was found in a gull pellet on one occasion. Birds that on their migratory journeys land exhausted on beaches in spring and autumn may be quickly dispatched by hungry gulls.

Adult herring gulls return to the breeding colony early in spring, and often meet up with last year's mate in the same territory. Both sexes join in building the nest, which is usually constructed of grass and seaweed. Always opportunists, herring gulls make use of all available natural habitats and quite a few which are man-made. On Walney Island I once made a list of unusual nest sites, including one within the circle of a car tyre washed up on the beach, one in an orange-box similarly deposited and one inside an abandoned wheelbarrow near a gravel pit. In some old offices once used by a saltworks there used to be a safe, its steel door hanging open on rusting hinges; inside, on a shelf, a gull sat firmly on its nest. Yet another nest was surrounded by three beer bottles (Mackeson, Bass No 1 and Newcastle Brown), obviously placed there deliberately. The clutch size is normally three, but two and four are recorded on occasions. The eggs vary in colour: they are usually buff with dark blotches, but I have found both light blue and very dark brown clutches. Occasionally a clutch varies from egg to egg. In fact the egg colour of most species varies a lot, but it is only in colonial species such as gulls and terns that enough clutches are seen close together for the variations to be appreciated. People who claim to identify all species purely from a cursory glance at an egg in the nest are to be mistrusted. Variations can lead to problems of identification, and the adults attending the nest should be studied to confirm the species. It is, for example, impossible to distinguish between the eggs of herring gulls and lesser black-backed gulls.

Herring gulls start to incubate once the first eggs are laid, and thus the hatching is staggered over a couple of days. Tinbergen's work has shown that parent birds quickly learn to recognise their offspring, and vice versa. Any chick straying from the area of its nest is quickly swallowed whole by an adult bird. They begin to attempt flight at about forty-five days, but they continue to beg food from their harassed parents until well into the autumn; I have even observed an immature gull begging food from an obviously unwilling adult in January. It was significant to see that the youngster was stabbing at the lower mandible of the adult's bill in the area of the red spot.

The Lesser Black-backed Gull

Together with the herring gull, this species (*Larus fuscus*) has caused biologists who specialise in classification endless sleepless nights. A definition of a species is one which breeds with other members of the species to produce fertile offspring. But it has been found that on the odd occasion herring gulls and lesser black-backed gulls have interbred and the resultant offspring have been fertile. Therefore some biologists insist that the two are really variations of the same species and should be described as sub-species or more accurately as a ring species. The majority, however, insist that the differences between the two are sufficiently distinct to warrant classifying them as different species, despite the odd record of interbreeding. Generally speaking the two keep apart, even on Walney Island where there are about equal numbers of each.

As already indicated the eggs cannot be distinguished from those of the herring gull, but the nests seem less substantial. Another interesting contrast is in the attitude of the adult birds to their young. Both herring-gull parents feed the young, but in the lesser black-backed gull only the female does so. She must do her job well, however, since the young can fly on or about the thirty-sixth day after hatching. Lesser black-backed gulls also differ in being mainly summer visitors, spending the winter in Portugal, Spain and north-west Africa. They do seem to have an increasing tendency to winter in Britain, but a high percentage of the lesser black-backed gull population is migratory.

The Greater Black-backed Gull

Larus marinus is the most powerful gull breeding in northern Europe, a large bird with huge bill and slow, measured wingbeat. It can be distinguished from the lesser black-backed gull not only by size but by the fact that its mantle (back) is black, as opposed to the smaller species' slate-grey colour. The greater black-backed gull tends to be more of a solitary nester than other gull species, and colonies of more than ten nests are unusual in Britain – though there are records of colonies of nearly 1,000 pairs in Orkney. They do, however, sometimes breed in small numbers in the midst of a colony of another gull species; they are, for instance, found on Walney Island in the midst of the herring and lesser black-backed gulls. They like to place their nest near a rock so that the bird which is not on incubation duty can stand guard. Three eggs are laid at three-day intervals and both parents share in the incubation, which begins with the second egg. The young fledge in about fifty days and during their first winter travel on average between 100 and 130 miles south; some reach the Iberian peninsula. Older birds tend to be much more sedentary in Britain, but careful work by ringers from other countries and sharp-eyed British amateur birdwatchers has shown that many Russian, Norwegian and Swedish birds winter in Britain. There are also a few records of Icelandic birds reaching our coastline in winter.

The Black-headed Gull

Larus ridibundus is the smallest of our resident gulls, and is extremely common both on the coast and inland. The inland movement in the winter has become very pronounced this century; it has been estimated that 200,000 may roost on the London reservoirs alone. The hood is chocolate-brown rather than black and it is purely a breeding plumage. The winter plumage, without the dark head, is still distinctive enough; the odd individual may retain fragments of the chocolate hood throughout the winter but in most cases the head is white with a brown smudge just behind the eye. The adult's legs and bill are red. The immature birds have brown mottling on the backs instead of the light grey of the adults and bill and legs are of a dullish yellow. Black-headed gulls, again, are vocal birds, but their notes are higher-pitched than those of the larger gulls.

The breeding habitat is extremely varied, ranging from seaside dunes and saltings to moorland pools and tarns. The bird's feeding techniques have been carefully studied in recent years. The voluminous literature shows just how versatile a bird this is. It has a hovering technique, 'hanging' over water and flopping down on to potential prey, often almost submerging in the process. After stabbing at its prey the gull struggles to rise from the waves to continue its hunting. It does this much more delicately than any of the larger gulls can manage, but compared to the splendidly athletic terns the performance is rather clumsy.

Another method of obtaining food is by bullying other species until they either drop their food or regurgitate the contents of their crop – a method known as kleptoparasitism. Many species are given this rough

110

Black-headed gull and chick (Leslie Jackman/Wildlife Picture Agency)

treatment: in the air black-headed gulls follow other gulls, terns and even herons; on fresh water they harass ducks, grebes and coots, and on the sea the lives of cormorants and sea ducks such as eiders and red-breasted mergansers are made miserable at times. I once watched a group of four black-headed gulls picking on a raft of eiders, and counted the number of attacks on drakes and the number of attacks on female eiders. Of the fifty attacks, forty-one were on males and only nine on females. This may be due to the fact that the drake is much lighter in colour and much easier to see as he approaches the surface with his food; the gulls can thus pinpoint his position and attack just when he is most vulnerable.

Apart from using the bludgeon the black-headed gull can on occasion feed in a most delicate manner, reminiscent of a swallow feeding on aerial insects. Sometimes on a warm summer's day, as the earth bakes in the heat, hot-air currents rise in waves, carrying light and unwary insects with them; at breeding time ants have wings and the males rise on these thermals in pursuit of the queen ant. The gulls wait, and on a still day you can hear their mandibles snapping as they open and close on the succulent insects. The gulls call in pleasure as they feed and the ant wings they reject float down as gently as snowflakes on a still winter night.

During the breeding season two or three eggs are laid, of a bluish-green ground-colour blotched with brown and grey. Incubation is shared by both parents. After about twenty-three days the young hatch, and after nearly thirty days of feeding by both parents they can fly; but as with other species of gull they continue to solicit food for some time afterwards.

Dune Slacks

Just as in the development of saltmarshes, there are depressions in a dune which fill with water; this is usually brackish but its salinity depends very much on the rainfall. These areas, the dune slacks (the origin is the Scandinavian *slaki*, damp hollow), are extremely rich. Their vegetation will vary much more than in the main dune systems and will largely depend upon man's activities. Common to most, however, will be creeping willow, sea milkwort and sea heath. Into these areas may come plants which like damp areas, such as marsh penny-wort, lesser spearwort, marsh marigold and marsh cinquefoil. Where there is standing water, in comes the common reed, yellow flag and burr reeds. If a fresh-water stream feeds into the dune slack, the parsley water dropwort will almost certainly be found. On Braunton Burrows in North Devon there are areas dominated by buckshorn plantain and hairy hawkbit; in some slacks the rush population dominates, mainly *Juncus maritimus* and *Juncus acutus*. At Roanhead dunes in Cumbria are large stands of early marsh orchid, creeping willow, yellow rattle and red rattle, and among these are found common spotted orchid, yellow wort, northern bedstraw, dune heleborine and meadowsweet.

There can be no doubt that the richer slacks contain wonderful plants, including marsh helleborine, round-leaved wintergreen and my own favourite flower, the delicate grass of Parnassus, now sadly absent from southern counties but still plentiful in the north and west. The Flemish botanist l'Obel (after whom the lobelia was named) fittingly christened this plant *gramen parnassi*, the grass of the holy mountain of Apollo. It is not a grass, of course, although it thrives amongst grasses, the white flowers shining forth like diamonds from a green setting. Five petals veined with green and tipped with yellow advertise a rich store of honey to the insects which busily hunt food and pollinate the plant in exchange for a meal. Grass of Parnassus was used by the old herbalists who called it (and many other plants) liverwort, boiling the leaves and using the concoction to treat liver complaints and 'settle the stomach'.

It is not only the plants, rich and sometimes rare, that attract the

112

Natterjack toad (E. C. M. Haes)

naturalist to dune slacks, for it is only here that all three of our native tailless amphibians can be found breeding. The frog and the common toad will both breed in dune slacks, provided the salinity of the standing water is not too high. If some salt is present, they may share their nuptial bed with the rare and declining natterjack toad.

The Natterjack
Bufo calamita is increasingly threatened by loss of habitat through drainage and land-reclamation schemes (as discussed in my book *The Making of the British Countryside*, David & Charles, 1981). It is definitely confined to coastal areas, and is mainly a nocturnal species, living in colonies. If there is too much disturbance in the area, then the whole colony migrates in search of somewhere more peaceful. Suitable areas are now scarce, and diminishing every year.

Using its short but powerful limbs, the natterjack excavates tunnels in the sand. The females are 10cm (4in) long, almost 2.5cm (1in) longer than their mates, but because of their short limbs neither sex can hop like other frogs and toads; one of their vernacular names is 'the running toad'. A conspicuous yellow line running down the middle of their backs is, like their gait, unique to this species.

In October or November, depending on temperature, the natterjacks begin their period of 'winter rigidity', emerging from it in February or early March. The breeding season is protracted, often lasting from April into July. In shallow pools of slightly salty water the eggs are laid in long strings, each of which may contain up to 4,000. Between the fifth and the tenth day they hatch into tadpoles, and then pass through a series of changes similar to those of the frog. The natterjack however completes its metamorphosis in about six weeks, much quicker than other amphibians. Biologists think this is an adaptation to life in a sand-dune system, where the shallow pools of spring and early summer tend to evaporate by early August, an event which would kill tadpoles, unable to breathe out of water. When the young emerge from the water they are like tiny editions of the adults, only about 1cm long. The animal is not in breeding condition until its fourth or even fifth summer, but like most amphibians can live a long time, sometimes reaching its fiftieth year.

The natterjack has another feature in common with other amphibians. Certain cells in the skin contain pigments that can be released to change the skin's colour so that it matches the surroundings and provides a perfect camouflage. This serves both to protect the animal from predators and to hide it while it lies in wait for its own prey. Its food consists of invertebrates, but only moving prey is selected and captured by the long sticky tongue which it flicks out with almost unnerving aim. I once had a most fascinating hour sitting on my favourite Cumbrian sand-dune system just after dawn on an August morning. A number of natterjacks were basking just where I expected them to be, facing east and soaking up the warming rays of the early sun. I spread a heap of blowfly- and mealworm-maggots around them and waited. Eight toads were soon gathered around my feet and I was totally ignored as they eagerly snapped up this unexpected and succulent breakfast.

It is difficult to tear yourself away from a dune slack but I urge you to do it (eventually!) and climb the steep hills of sand towards the land. Then stand atop a stable dune or the slopes of woodland marking the end-product of the 'sand-dune succession' and look back towards the sea where the whole sequence began. Watch the tide ebb uncover what seems to be a desert of endless sand and mud. Look through binoculars and watch the birds feeding; close your eyes and listen to their calls. Here, then, is no desert but a rich harvest of nutritious food. Retrace your steps to the tideline, take a few items of equipment with which to dig and sieve the sand, and a whole new world will open up before you.

114

6
Sandy Shores

A sandy shore is, in my view, at its best in late autumn and early winter. At this time the hordes of human holidaymakers have gone and the birds have returned from breeding, the majority having completed their moult. The high equinoctial tides have deposited their treasures on the strandline and there is no strong hot sunshine to bleach the exquisite colours of the shells. Gone too are the children who enjoy, and who would dare begrudge them, collecting the strange 'cast-ups' and incorporating them into their castles. My finest hours are spent on the beaches during December mornings as dawn breaks to greet an ebbing tide and take the edge off the freezing air, and on the sand and mudflats are the waders, probing their bills deep in search of food.

By far the commonest large wader, and the easiest to recognise, is the curlew, but on occasions it may be joined by the whimbrel, bar-tailed godwit and black-tailed godwit. With practice the four species can readily be distinguished, especially if the points noted in the diagram overleaf are memorised or copied into a field notebook.

In Chapter 3 I referred to the redshank family of waders, but other species are also common, especially the smaller dunlin and the sanderling which is much paler than the dunlin although the two are of similar size. The dunlin averages some 17.5cm (7in) and the sanderling 20cm (8in). There is also a third very common wader, the knot, which is a larger bird altogether, some 25cm (10in). All three species, especially the dunlin, are renowned for the sheer brilliance of their co-ordinated flying; many hundreds of birds can sweep and turn, dive and stall, as if all triggered by the same switch. Their pale underparts reflect the silvery rays of the low winter sun like a heliograph, the flash being almost as regular as a metronome as the flock goes through its paces. Eventually, however, their energy reserves run down and the flock lands and begins to feed; now the wary birdwatcher can see that the bill of the dunlin is very long and either straight or very slightly decurved: an examination of a number of individuals will reveal some variation in both length and shape. Such a large bill on such a small bird may go some way towards explaining its slightly hump-backed appearance.

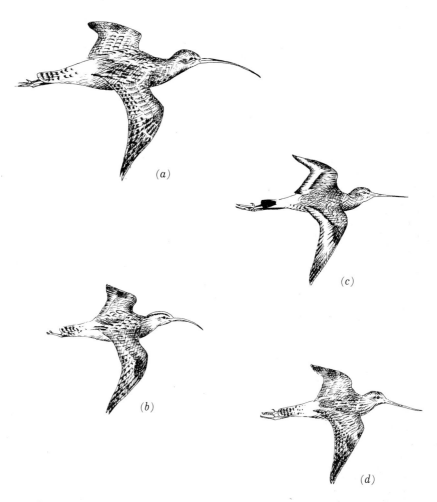

(a) Curlew; (b) whimbrel, with line over the eye; (c) black-tailed godwit, with white wing bar; (d) bar-tailed godwit

Strong sunlight reflects from the plumage and reveals its brownish upper parts and greyish breast, and if by good fortune sanderlings are present as well, their much whiter plumage will be obvious. The patient ornithologist will keep watching as the birds fly: though a whitish wing-bar will be seen on the dunlin it is much less conspicuous than on the sanderling, where the wing-bar is one of the most prominent features. Look also at the tails of the flying waders. Both sanderling and dunlin have white edges to the tail with a black central portion which is very easily seen. The knot has no dark centre to the tail, and although there is

Walney Island, Cumbria (English Tourist Board)

a wing-bar it is much less conspicuous than even the dunlin's, in some
individuals not visible at all. Other differences are readily observed
when the knot lands, for as well as being a much larger bird it is also
much greyer. The bill is straight and comparatively shorter than in the
dunlin, and the legs are shorter in comparison to body-size than is usual
in waders, thus giving the knot a very dumpy appearance.

All three species feed on the sand and mudflats when the tide is out, but also tend to chase ebbing waves, thus catching crustaceans, worms and shellfish, and retreating in the face of the following wave. Some say that the knot earned its name of *Calidris canutus* from its habit of dicing with death in the shape of the sea as did King Canute of old, although Henry Massingham in his *Birds of the Seashore*, published in 1931, disputed this, pointing out that 'the name takes its true origin from the low monosyllabic cry – knut, knut, though on alighting from a communal flight the birds will often burst, in the manner of starlings, into a soft and limpid conversazione.'

Although these waders are seen at their collective best during the shorter months of the year, they are also interesting at other times. True, there will not be huge hordes of gyrating birds, but the odd individual in full breeding plumage is worth seeing. The head, neck and upper breast of the sanderling become delicately shaded with light chestnut, in beautiful contrast to the belly which remains white. The dunlin and the knot both sport chestnut areas; in the knot the head and underparts are liberally sprinkled, and the back is chestnut mottled with black. The breeding dunlin can be distinguished from both its relatives by having a chestnut-and-black back and also a prominent black patch on the breast. Over 6,000 pairs of dunlin breed in Britain, where they show a preference for dry upland moors, but neither the sanderling nor the knot breed with us. In winter our estuaries carry over 500,000 dunlin and 350,000 knot, and over 6,000 sanderling twinkle along our sandy beaches like clockwork toys; what energy reserves these vast numbers of birds must require.

The reserves, in the form of crustaceans, molluscs and worms, in their turn depend upon other animals, and more indirectly upon plants making food from the energy provided by sunlight. The surfaces of both sandy and muddy shores are too unstable to support large forms of plant life, so we must rely upon the evidence of microscopists who look closely into the detailed texture of the substrate. On a sandy shore, quartz is the main constituent, although other rock fragments are also present. Sand particles are defined as those with a diameter between 0.02 and 2.0mm, smaller grains making up a mud and larger ones constituting a shingle. Between the sand particles are microscopic animals and plants and it is this 'interstitial' fauna and flora, assisted a little by the marine plankton which ebbs and flows above it, which forms the base of the vast pyramid supporting the rest of the shore animals. The larger forms can be studied by either one of two methods, or better still by a combination of both. By examining the driftline you will find the bodies of animals which have died below the surface and then been scoured out of their subterranean sarcophagi by the relentless sea. The other, and in many ways, the more scientific method is to follow the ebbing tide and dig into the sand, then sieve out the animals.

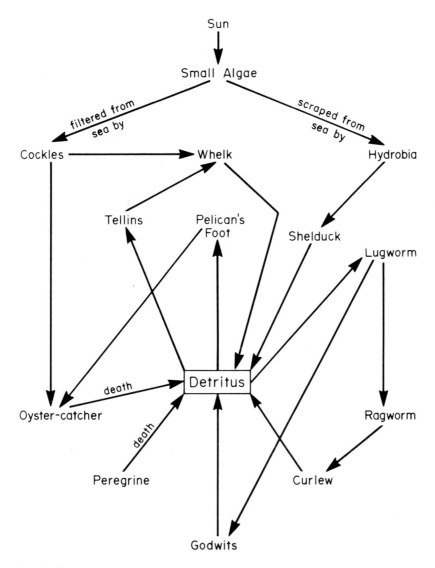

Sandy-shore food web

Looking at the driftline will reveal many forms of shell, but it is only by digging that the vast numbers of worms will be revealed.

The most obvious inhabitants of the driftline area will be the so-called shellfish; they are part of a large animal phylum, the molluscs. They are soft-bodied invertebrates, most of which protect their vulnerable parts within a protective shell secreted by the outer layer of the specialised cells which make up the soft body often called the

Tideline after a storm. The large fish is a wrasse, the large shells are otter shells; there is also a burrowing starfish and rednose cockle (Leslie Jackman/Wildlife Picture Agency)

mantle. The phylum is divided into five groups, of which only the first two are likely to be prolific on sandy shores. The gastropoda, sometimes called univalves, have their bodies enclosed in a single shell; bivalves have a shell in two halves, linked by a strong muscle. The Amphineura or chitons are found on rocky shores (Chapter 7); and both the Scaphopoda (tropical tusk shells) and the Cephalopoda, which includes the cuttlefish, squids and octopuses, live well below the tidal range. The shell of the cuttlefish (*Sepia officinalis*) is often washed up on the shore, and is much appreciated by cage birds; it was once collected for this purpose, since 'cuttlebone' is a valuable source of grit for them.

A stroll along a sandy beach to collect shells, especially after a high tide in spring or autumn, will produce a varied and interesting collection. Among the univalves found are likely to be actaeon (*Actaeon tornatilis*), common necklace shell, common wendletrap, large top shell, and the tower or spire shell. Bivalves will include the pullet carpet shell, banded carpet shell, and striped venus. If the shore has muddy expanses, then other species will find suitable niches, including the peppery furrow

Harvesting cockles, Gower, South Wales (Leslie Jackman/Wildlife Picture Agency)

shell, great scallop or clam – which can be up to 15cm (6in) across – the smaller queen scallop, the common oyster, the blunt gaper and the sand gaper. All these may be found on the strandline, but the dominant bivalves there will almost certainly be cockles, tellins and razors.

Cockles

The surface of these well-known and handsome shells is covered with prominent ridges and short spines. The thick valves are joined by a tough brown ligament. On sandy shores, two out of the eleven British species are particularly common. The edible cockle (*Cerastoderma edule*) is found close to and even on the surface; and when high spring tides expose the lower regions of the shore the larger prickly cockle (*Acanthocardia echinata*) is found in some numbers. The 11cm ($4\frac{1}{2}$in) diameter shell is about three times the size of the common cockle and there are more and larger spines on its surface. In the living animal, the foot of the prickly cockle is pink, that of the edible cockle yellow.

Cockles, being shallow burrowers, have short siphons fringed with tentacles, and also have simple eyes that obviously help them determine

121

Oyster catcher, much feared by cockle fishermen, incubates a clutch of three eggs (Leslie Jackman/Wildlife Picture Agency)

their depth beneath the surface. The inhalant siphon scrapes the surface, drawing in a current of water, from which planktonic food and respiratory gases are extracted; the exhalant siphon pumps out the nutrient- and oxygen-depleted water, to which has been added waste products such as urine and carbon dioxide. The fact that cockles are so exposed means that they face almost continuous threats from predators, and the main method of escape involves the use of the enormous muscle called the foot; this in no way resembles a mammalian foot. The prickly cockle can push its foot down on to the sand suddenly and violently straighten it out and thereby leap a distance of about 20cm (8in) in order to escape hunting birds or starfish. The edible cockle is not so powerful, but for its size is quite a creditable long-jumper.

In suitable areas between the tide marks, cockle populations can be staggering: in South Wales an area was surveyed and the total there was estimated at 460 million individuals! It is as well that they are so prolific since there is no shortage of hungry predators, from starfish such as *Astropecten irregularis* underneath the sand, to oyster catchers above it

– not to mention voracious members of its own phylum, such as the necklace shell (*Natica alderi*), which bores gimlet-like through shells and rasps away at the tender flesh within. Examine a number of shells along the strandline and in some you will find a neat hole drilled by this master-craftsman.

Not only predators reduce the cockle population at times, since it is concentrated close enough to the surface to be scoured out by winter storms and boiled in its own juices by the strength of the summer sun during periods of neap tides. The natural world, however, evolved in fluctuating conditions that bring troughs and peaks in populations. No bivalve has more reproductive virility than the cockle, although it must be rivalled by the tellin, which probably has an advantage in not being on the human menu.

Tellins

There are twenty-four British species in the Tellinidae family; they usually have thin fragile shells, flattish in shape and often colourful. In contrast to the cockles, tellins are deep burrowers, having one extremely long siphon and another slightly shorter; the former is protruded above the sand when the tide is in and sweeps around in a circle, drawing in water and any material suspended in it like an animated vacuum cleaner. The shorter siphon serves, as usual, as a wastepipe. This system is termed deposit feeding.

Three species are very common around our coasts, the thin tellin (*Tellina tenuis*) and the bean-like tellin (*Tellina fabula*) which both seem fond of sandy bases, and in muddy situations the Baltic tellin (*Macoma balthica*). The name of this species reflects the fact that its range extends into the low-saline waters of the Baltic. In the thin tellin, both valves of the shell are glossy, and although they show growth-lines there is no other form of sculpturing. The creamy-coloured bean-like tellin has a much more pointed anterior end, and looked at under a hand lens oblique sculpturing can be detected on the right valve. Both these species measure about 2cm (about ¾in) across the shell, but the Baltic tellin is larger, 2.5cm (1in) in diameter. These shells are also very colourful, a delightful yellow or a flushed pink. This is one of the most powerful of the tellins; it can move more easily through muds, and finds conditions much to its liking in Swansea Bay, Morecambe Bay, the Duddon and the Solway.

Also included in the tellin family are three other mud-lovers, the banded wedgeshell (*Donax vittatus*), peppery furrow shell (*Scrobicularia plana*) and egg razorshell (*Pharus legumen*). This latter species (sometimes called the jack-knife clam) must not be confused with the true razorshells which share this rich habitat. Its shell resembles a cut-throat razor, but the two valves are hinged in the middle.

Razorshells

These are easily recognised: the two halves of the long thin shell are joined at one end by a hinge. There are four similar species which bury themselves vertically in the sand, and if disturbed by wind or potential predator use their powerful foot driven by hydrostatic pressure to disappear downwards with remarkable speed. The species found commonly are the pod razor (*Ensis siliqua*), the sword razors (*Ensis ensis* and *Ensis arcuatus*) and the grooved razor (*Solen marginatus*), which shows a preference for muddy shores.

The pod razorshell measures 23cm (9in) and is the largest and commonest of the razorshells. The two valves are both straight on both edges, in contrast to the sword razors. *Ensis ensis* is 12cm ($4\frac{3}{4}$in) long and curved on both edges; *Ensis arcuatus* is 15cm (6in) long and the shells *are curved on one side only*. The grooved razor has a prominent groove near the anterior margin and measures 12cm ($4\frac{3}{4}$in).

Another bivalve that must be mentioned is the otter shell (*Lutraria lutraria*), which has valves measuring up to 15cm (6in) and is therefore easily seen lying on the driftline. The living animal is found off shore, snug in its burrow some 30cm (12in) down in the sand. The siphons are very long indeed, often twice as long as the shell, and wave about above the surface whenever the tide is in. A look at the inside of an empty valve reveals a prominent triangular pit marking the site of the very powerful ligament which holds the shell together, and other impressions can be found marking the positions of the muscles which once operated the impressive siphons. Otter shells are often found washed up alongside those of the common whelk or buckie.

The Whelk

The dull whitish shell of *Buccinum undatum* is made up of broad ridges or whorls called varices, with narrower spiral ridges crossing them. Whelks can reach a height of 10cm (4in), but the majority found on the shore are smaller than this, the giants being found in quite deep water. This is the largest of Britain's gastropod molluscs and is well known to the general public because, with the periwinkle (*Littorina littorea*), it is edible – although the flesh is tough and needs a lot of boiling. Whelks are caught by dredging the shallow water in which they pursue their own varied prey. They will take other molluscs, either living or dead, often employing 'intelligent' strategies to unlock their shells. They have been known to perch on top of an oyster's shell until it opens its valves, then quickly insert their proboscis and gobble up the soft nutritious flesh within.

As well as whelk shells the strandline may provide the beachcomber with large bundles of whelk eggs. They are laid in large capsules which are fastened together with a glue-like substance, the mass being anchored to rocks or the seabed itself. The young hatch and force their way out, and eventually the huge sponge-like bundle of spent egg-cases is washed ashore. Just occasionally small living specimens are stranded after a storm, and if these are doused with sea water a siphon will be seen projecting from the shell; this structure is formed from the mantle and acts like a suction pump to draw water into the mantle cavity and over a taste receptor, technically known as the osphradium. Thus the whelk is able to locate its food by sampling the water. The siphonal canal is an important feature to the taxonomist, because its structure differs in the various species. We also have smaller whelks, such as the oyster drill or sting winkle (*Ocenebra erinacea*) and the netted dog whelk (*Nassarius reticulatus*) to delight the shell collector.

The Pelican's Foot

In everyone's top ten, however, would be the pelican's-foot shell (*Aporrhais pes-pelecani*). These were once eagerly collected by the Victorians and used to decorate the frames of pictures and the lids of boxes, a craft which still persists in some areas. The genus *Aporrhais* is principally centred on the Atlantic and does not extend any further than the Mediterranean. The pelican's foot lives best in gravelly sand; soft mud tends to block its respiratory gills. A second member of the genus, *Aporrhais serressiana*, has a more delicate but much sharper shell which can live in muddier and softer substrates without having its breathing surfaces fouled: the pair provide yet another example of the biological niche system in action.

Both species live offshore and feed on detritus sucked from the seabed by the vacuum-cleaner arrangement of twin siphons, although some workers have suggested that this may just be a respiratory current, feeding being solely the function of the extensible radula which scrapes food from the surface of the sand or mud. The animal moves by extending its powerful foot and once this is anchored the rest of the body is pulled towards it. This area then becomes 'home' until the food supply is exhausted, and the cumbersome procedure is repeated. When ripped unceremoniously from the shallow seabed by storms, the shells are thrown on to the shore, when the reason for the vernacular name of pelican's foot can easily be understood by looking just below the shell opening. From here radiates a series of lines looking just like a bird's footprint.

The Marine Snail, Hydrobia

If pelican's foot is the most famous shell found on a sandy beach then surely the marine snail *Hydrobia ulvae* (Laver spire shell) must be the least well known, until recently not even having a vernacular name, despite being arguably the most important univalve.

The tiny cone-shaped shells seldom reach more than 0.6cm (about ¼in), and the odd specimen approaching 1cm (just under ½in) is usually found to be twisted and deformed by the presence of parasitic trematode worms. What they lack in size the hydrobians make up in numbers; at times their presence may make whole sandy or muddy banks look granulated in texture. Populations in the order of 50,000 per square metre have been estimated from the Tamar in Cornwall, parts of Morecambe Bay and the Duddon Estuary and in the Firths of Clyde and Forth. Most animals living within the range of the tide have to gear their feeding strategy to its rhythm and this means that they can only feed at certain times. *Hydrobia ulvae* is able to feed at any state of tide, and this may be the main reason for its dominance. When it is covered by the sea it forms a mucus raft which not only keeps it afloat but also acts as a sticky net to trap plankton. When the tide has ebbed the 'raft' is deflated and the Spire shell crawls about the wet surface until it finally dries; then it burrows into the mud or sand to avoid desiccation. All the time the tentacles search the surface for detritus and microscopic diatoms.

Reproduction occurs during the summer, the females depositing their eggs on any available solid surface including the shells of their own species. The larval stage (technically called a veliger) is very short, and afterwards the molluscs settle on the mud surface.

Here they form an important item on the menu of many birds, especially the shelduck, for whom *Hydrobia* may be 90 per cent of the total food intake. At the moment this bird's dependence upon what amounts to a monoculture is not a problem, but should any disaster similar to that which affected the eel grass (*Zostera marina*), discussed in Chapter 4, overtake the marine snail, if favoured estuaries were ever 'barraged' or affected by oil spill, then the very survival of the shelduck would be threatened. It is not part of a naturalist's job to 'cry wolf', but it is incumbent upon those who love our wildlife to highlight species such as this which could be particularly vulnerable.

The Shelduck

Few European ducks are as spectacular to look at as *Tadorna tadorna*. Unusually, the two sexes look similar, although the male is rather larger and brighter and has a red knob at the base of the bill, particularly obvious during the breeding season. These distinctions can be easily observed since the birds pair for life and tend to hold territories, both for breeding and for feeding, so the two are seen close together on the sand-flats. It is during the vigorous defence of these hydrobia-rich areas that the normally silent birds make their presence felt, and it is perhaps surprising to hear the male's soft whistle drowned by the deeper, somewhat raucous 'ark-ark-ark' of his mate.

Though you may see shelduck feeding on the shore, the sand dunes are by far their most favoured breeding sites. There is nothing that the duck finds more to her liking than a cosy rabbit-hole which she often wants so badly that she will evict the rightful owners. The male plays no part in the choice of nesting site but faithfully guards the territory while his mate is sitting. The average clutch is about eleven but there are regular reports of up to thirty-two being found, incubated by a single female, in nests where several ducks have obviously deposited their eggs. This 'cuckoo-type' behaviour must have a definite advantage when nesting sites are at a premium. Even after hatching the communal spirit continues, as crèches of young birds are tended by a few adults. This must have great survival value when adult birds die from natural causes or are shot. Crèching is also useful when adults feel the urge to begin their unique moult-migration journey. By far the majority of our shelducks – and some 13,000 pairs breed in Britain – undertake the arduous trip to the Heligoland Bight in West Germany purely to moult, and are joined here by other European members of the species: at times up to 100,000 individuals moult there. But about 4,000 shelducks, probably Irish breeders, moult in Bridgwater Bay, Somerset, and a smaller flock has recently been noted moulting near Aberdeen.

Wherever they moulted, shelducks begin to drift back to their breeding areas during the autumn, where they feed greedily, usually on hydrobia, and quickly build up muscle and body fat. I look forward at this time to watching these lovely wildfowl, heads swinging from side to side through the wet mud and shallow pools of saline water, bills sieving out food. Sometimes droplets of liquid drop from their nostrils catching the sun and shining like dewdrops, demonstrating the perfect functioning of the salt glands (see Chapter 2). Although as we have seen the marine snail is the most important food item, a nice juicy worm will never come amiss and there is certainly no shortage of these on the shore.

Worms of a Sandy Shore

Worms abound on all our coasts, whatever their nature, varying in size from tiny creatures which can hardly be seen with the naked eye to huge creatures longer than a metre (39in)! Most are so unlike the common earthworm (*Lumbricus terrestris*) that they are not even recognised as members of the roundworm phylum – the annelids. The majority live beneath the surface of the sand, but one species produces tangible evidence of its considerable presence: this is the lugworm or lobworm (*Arenicola marina*), whose coiled castings are often conspicuous on sandy shores. Those high on the beach are much smaller than those close to the low-water mark, which suggests that when an individual

Sand mason (left) and lugworm (right)

outgrows its burrow it emerges on a full tide, swims seawards for a while and then rapidly constructs a new home. Though the lugworm lives in a burrow like its earthworm relative, it is a much more sedentary species, seldom leaving its tube.

A close look around the castings will show a small saucer-shaped depression; between the two, the sand is penetrated by a U-shaped tunnel, its walls lined with mucus and often quite firm. The head faces the depression, the tail end obviously being responsible for the coiled casting. Like the earthworm, *Arenicola* feeds by ingesting material through the mouth, digesting food particles and finally ejecting the residue. It feeds continually while the tide is out, drawing sand into its tunnel, so the depression deepens, but the force of the incoming sea pushes in more sand with a fresh food supply. The oxygen-rich water required for respiration is periodically drawn in from the tail end and circulated over the gill system.

Lugworms are popular bait with sea anglers, but of great interest to marine biologists, since they are easily dug up and 'transplant well' into laboratories. If they are placed in a U tube made of glass their activities can be closely watched, and lugworms taken from the shore still show their greatest mobility at the times corresponding to their home tidal rhythms. Here, then, is yet another example of a biological clock. The glass vessel also allows the external anatomy of the lugworm to be seen clearly, the body is divided into three parts, its girth gradually reducing

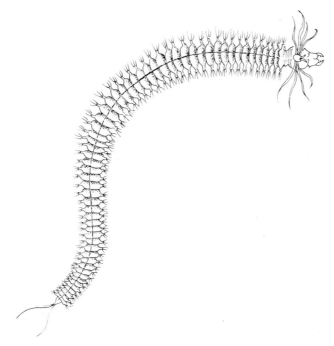

Ragworm

from the head through the middle region to the tail. The head and middle regions have retractable bristles which enable *A renicola* to grip the sides of its burrow and move up and down. Each segment in the middle region also has a pair of small feather-like gills.

The lugworm's sedentary feeding method is in complete contrast to the active, often ferocious, hunting technique of the ragworms – also popular bait with sea anglers. One of the largest species is the handsome green ragworm (*Nereis virens*), 20cm (8in) long and some individuals are so powerful that their jaws can inflict a painful nip to the careless human hand. All species have bodies divided into something like 100 obvious segments, with outgrowths sprouting from the sides of all except the first few behind the head. These parapodia, as they are called, consist of dorsal and ventral portions, each of which bears specialised bristle-like structures called chaetae. The parapodia carry out several vital functions, such as gripping the sand when the tide is out, or swimming through the water when it is in, and they also considerably increase the surface area over which respiratory gases can reach the liberal blood supply which flows through them. The big head, clearly distinct from the body, bears simple eyes and antenna-like tentacles which are efficient organs with which to sight their prey, which is grabbed and dispatched by strong jaws. There are several species of

129

these 'sea centipedes' so named because of their superficial resemblance to land centipedes, the myriapoda. All these nereids are mainly carnivorous although they do not despise the odd 'veg' to go with their meat.

Another common species is the red-line ragworm (*Nereis diversicolor*); the long line down its back is the dorsal blood vessel, which is conspicuous against the rest of the pale brown body. As this attractive animal glides across the surface of the wet mud, its 15cm (6in) body often reflects sunlight, and the animated rainbow so produced accounts for the specific name 'diversicolor'.

Both lugworms and nereids are obviously, even from the most superficial sighting, annelid worms, but this is certainly not the case with the sea mouse (*Aphrodite aculeata*). It is not all that common on the shore, but is bound to be spotted from time to time by beachcombers with the eye for the unusual. Its carcase is often deposited on the shore after a heavy storm has flushed it from its shallow burrow or surprised it while on a feeding sortie in search of the carrion which forms the bulk of the diet. The sea mouse looks like a large, fat, hairy slug and it is only when it is turned on to its back that the body segments and bristle-type parapodia can be seen. The whole of the upper surface and the sides are covered by hair-like structures which have a wonderful green and golden iridescent hue; since the sea mouse can reach lengths of 10cm (4in) it is a most impressive creature.

The last annelid worm to be discussed here, the sand mason (*Lanice conchilega*), is often overlooked. A walk along a sandy shore at low water often reveals heaps of material resembling short bits of stick, and if sheltered spots under piers are examined the living animals will be found sticking upright like small posts in the sand. The tube is made from sand grains, pieces of shell or even hardened mud bound together by mucus secreted from the skin of the worm. In these 30cm (12in) 'houses' lives a sand mason, which occasionally pokes its head out and extends a number of tentacles which gather organic debris from the sand or mud surface. The sand mason is difficult to detach from its tube, but if this can be carefully accomplished the annelid – usually consisting of about 150 segments – can be examined, and a most attractive animal it is.

A walk along a sandy shore is also likely to yield many other fascinating objects, including the empty tests of the heart urchin and the discarded egg-cases of two of our most common sharks which live off shore.

The Heart Urchin (Echinocardium cordatum)
This is often a common inhabitant of the sand near low-tide level. It shows many structural and behavioural differences from the more

typical urchins living on rocky coasts (see Chapter 7). The nearly-white shell or test is quite fragile and soon loses its spines when buffeted by the sea – the empty tests are often called 'sea potatoes'. The animal's preferred habitat is the middle and lower regions of the shore, and it is particularly attracted to clean sand into which it burrows to a depth of about 10cm (4in). It is not spherical like rocky-shore urchins but heart-shaped and thus a much more efficient burrower. As all members of the echinoderm phylum, it moves by means of structures called tube feet, which can be extended by hydrostatic pressure through holes in the grooves on the test. There is a sucker at the end of each tube foot, and once anchored the tube feet can be shortened by a reduction in the hydrostatic pressure. The suckers hold the animal firmly and the body is thus dragged forward. Urchins have five rows of these tube feet, thus clearly showing their strong evolutionary link with the five-armed starfish. In the sea potato, oxygen is carried down the burrow by means of two extra-long tube feet protruding from the anterior groove. These form a funnel, strengthened by mucus, and tiny hairs called cilia beat to produce a current which draws in sand grains, from which the creature's food is scraped. The system also brings in oxygen. Waste carbon dioxide, urine and faeces are discharged – again driven by cilia – via a second funnelling system, a 'sanitary tube' at the rear of the body. To find fresh food supplies, heart urchins shift about quite a lot, and they are gregarious – a habit which during their breeding season, June to August of their second year, ensures that sperm and eggs meet at the right time. The larvae spend some while drifting about in the plankton, then settle down on the sand and build the first of many burrows. Huge populations of the heart urchin exist as is shown by the quantities of empty tests cast up on sandy beaches, especially in late summer and early autumn, where they often lie alongside the egg-cases of dogfish and skates.

British 'Sharks'
Broadly speaking, fish can be divided into cartilaginous and bony types, the former being by far the more primitive, and amongst the earliest vertebrates to evolve; they are commonly called sharks, and many of them have interesting breeding strategies. The common spotted dogfish (*Scyliorhinus canicula*) is quite small, as sharks go, not usually exceeding 70cm (28in) in length or 2kg ($4\frac{1}{2}$lb) in weight, but it is abundant in numbers. Male and female are of equal size. After they come together to breed, most often in spring, the female lays her fertilised eggs within leathery, brownish oblong cases: long thin threads straggle from each corner, tangling round rocks or seaweed and thus providing anchorage. The eggs take just over 150 days to hatch, the young biting their way from their prisons when about 10cm (4in) long.

The abandoned egg-cases may end up on the beach – as the familiar 'mermaids' purses'. The purses of the common dogfish are about 5cm (2in) long, those of the greater spotted dogfish (*Scyliorhinus stellaris*) about twice that size.

The rays, which are large flat 'sharks', also lay their eggs in mermaids' purses, the commonest being those of the common skate (*Raja batis*). This is a deep-water species, less common around the English Channel than in the Irish Sea. It can reach a length of 2m (nearly 7ft) and weigh up to 180kg (about 400lb). The purses can be up to 15cm (6in) long, 7.5cm (3in) wide. The colour is almost black, and there are no long threads as on dogfish egg-capsules; the horny spines on the corners serve the same anchoring function.

This chapter concludes as it began with a description of a species which we know exists because we find evidence of its presence washed up on the strandline. There is little or no opportunity for most of us to study sea potatoes or dogfish in their natural habitat. Amongst the pools of rocky shores, however, we have easy access to a magnificent marine aquarium, fully stocked with living creatures.

7
Rocky Shores

Patella to the rock adheres
Nor of the raging tempest fears
The most tremendous power;
And though assail'd on every side
Close to her guardian will abide
Her strength, her fortress and her pride
Her never failing tower.

Sarah Hoare, *Poems on Conchology and Botany*, 1831

Nowhere can the sheer might of the sea be better observed than on a rocky shore. When looking at saltmarshes and sand dunes we saw the zonation of plant life by beginning at the low-water mark and from there working gradually inland. Rocky shores reveal an equally obvious zonation, of animals as well as plants, but this is best explained by waiting for a full spring tide, and following the ebb towards the low-water mark. The tide retreating over the uneven rocks will leave behind fascinating rock-pools, and birds will pick their way among the tangle of weeds in search of food.

Plant Zonation

Few flowering plants are able to survive between the tide lines. Their role in this inhospitable region is taken by primitive plants, the algae; the large marine members of this phylum are the 'seaweeds'. Their bodies are not organised into leaves, stems and roots, but are compact units called fronds, anchored to rock or other solid objects by structures called holdfasts. They do contain chlorophyll, and can manufacture essential food by photosynthesis, but the green colouring may be masked by other pigments; thus the phylum may be roughly classified by colour. There are red, yellow, blue-green and brown algae, in addition to smaller types which float in open water and make up the phyloplankton. It is the brown seaweeds that are dominant on and zoned along the rocky shore; the greens grow beneath them or near the high-water mark and the reds often occur in deep water or in rock-pools

133

Holdfasts of Laminaria digitata *at low tide* (Leslie Jackman/Wildlife Picture Agency)

where, aided by the buoyancy provided by the sea, they spread into some of the most beautiful life forms found in the sea.

Among the browns are some half-dozen species, spread from high to low water. The precise make-up and zone boundaries varies from beach to beach and with the steepness of the slope, but the basic pattern remains the same.

Channelled Wrack Zone
Pelvetia canaliculata has short, branched fronds that curl inwards along the margins, the feature that gives it its name. A plant right on the high-tide line must obviously spend most of its time out of water, and especially when exposed to hot sun it can lose up to 70 per cent of its moisture. It then becomes black and folds inwards, which helps to reduce further water loss. As soon as the frond is covered by the sea it quickly expands and its natural brown colour returns. It is this capacity to cope with drought and occasional soakings in sea water that allows

134

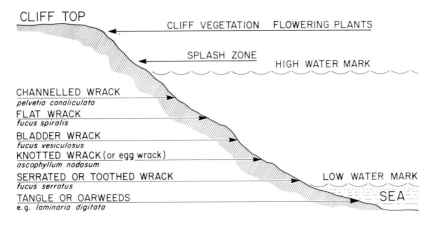

CLIFF TOP

CLIFF VEGETATION   FLOWERING PLANTS

SPLASH ZONE
HIGH WATER MARK

CHANNELLED WRACK
pelvetia canaliculata
FLAT WRACK
fucus spiralis
BLADDER WRACK
fucus vesiculosus
KNOTTED WRACK (or egg wrack)
ascophyllum nodosum
SERRATED OR TOOTHED WRACK
fucus serratus
TANGLE OR OARWEEDS
e.g. laminaria digitata

LOW WATER MARK

SEA

Zonation of seaweeds

the channelled wrack to dominate the shore from just below the splash zone; at times it even mingles with the flowering plants on the cliff edge and the landward end of the shore, such as thrift and sea plantain.

Flat Wrack Zone

At its seaward end, channelled wrack merges with the zone of the flat wrack (*Fucus spiralis*). The flat fronds of this plant are some 30cm (12in) long and 1cm (under half an inch) across. Each frond has an obvious midrib, smooth edges and branches into two at the tip. At the ends of these branches are structures called receptacles, the orange-brown reproductive organs typical of the brown seaweeds. These plants are hermaphrodite, so both male and female discharge their gametes (reproductive cells) into the ebbing tide, ensuring a wide distribution for them. Flat wrack can stand exposure for up to 80 per cent of the time, and its area of dominance is only slowly taken over by either the bladder wrack or knotted wrack; on occasions there is a co-dominant zone, shared by these two species.

Bladder Wrack and Knotted Wrack Zone

Fucus vesiculosus, the bladder wrack, is perhaps the best known of all seaweeds, easily recognised by the prominent air-bladders arranged in pairs along the fronds. Their function is to keep the plant floating at full tide, so that it gets plenty of light to carry on making the food it needs.

The knotted wrack (*Ascophyllum nodosum*) can be distinguished by the lack of a midrib and by having larger but single bladders – from these it is sometimes known as egg wrack. The plant's holdfast is so strong that if it is pulled up, the heavy stone to which it is attached may have to come too. Storm-force seas may wrench both together from

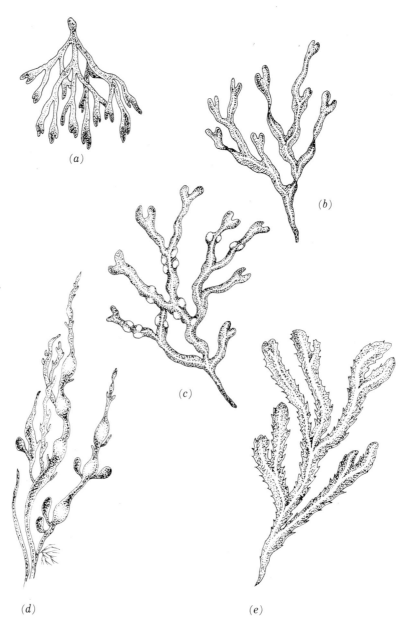

(a) Channelled wrack; (b) flat wrack; (c) bladder wrack; (d) knotted wrack; (e) serrated (or saw) wrack

their moorings and transport them for a considerable distance.

The relative distribution of bladder wrack and knotted wrack depends to some extent on how exposed a beach may be: the former species can withstand considerable buffeting, but egg wrack is a plant of more sheltered waters.

Serrated or Toothed Wrack Zone

The next obvious zone is dominated by *Fucus serratus*, the serrated or toothed wrack, found on the lower part of the shore. Its fronds are flat, like those of flat wrack, but larger and tougher, with prominent serrated margins – and no bladders at all, so its zone boundary is an obvious one. It is also one of the commonest of all our seaweeds, covering the rocks near the low-water line with a dense mat of slippery vegetations. Its receptacles take a different pattern, being spread like blisters over the tips of the fronds; male organs are much brighter orange than female organs. Serrated wrack grows where it will be covered with sea water for most of the time, so it rarely dries out – indeed its low tolerance of desiccation is the factor that prevents it from advancing up the beach. Its lower limit is the area below low water where the tide merges with the open sea: here it must yield dominance to the weed that occupies the final seaweed zone on the shore, the tangleweed or *Laminaria*.

Laminaria Zone

There are four common British tangleweeds, also known as kelps or oarweeds. In three of them the frond is drawn out into a fingerlike process. This gives the scientific name to *Laminaria digitata*, a long flexible species that shows structural variation in response to its environmental conditions: the greater the exposure, the more 'fingers' it seems to possess.

Laminaria hyperborea is a similar species, but the stem (known as the stipe) is less flexible so that the plant stands upright enough to stick out of the water at low tide, while being totally submerged at the flood.

Sea belt (*Laminaria saccharina*) shares this position just below low water with the two oarweeds, but is also found in rock-pools. This is the plant sometimes used as 'the poor man's barometer', the belief being that if a piece of it is hung up at home it will become dry and brittle when good weather is on the way, swollen and succulent as rain approaches. As it dries out, sea belt exudes a sticky, sweet-tasting liquid. The fronds are up to a maximum of 1.5 metres (5ft) long, and about 15cm (6in) wide.

The fourth species of the *Laminaria* zone, dabberlocks (*Alaria esculenta*), is easily recognised, the only oarweed with a prominent midrib. It is commoner on Scottish than English or Welsh coasts.

Plants so readily available in huge quantities have of course been

137

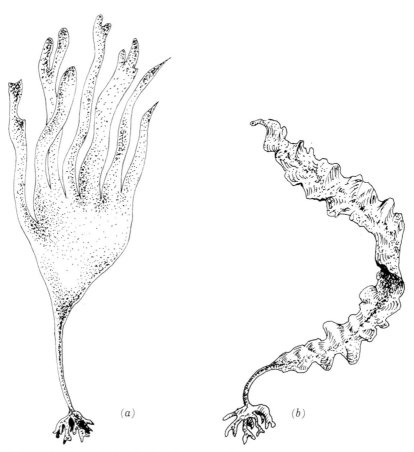

(a) Laminaria digitata; (b) Laminaria saccharina

tried by humans as sources of food. Many seaweeds have formed vital additions to the diet of people living near a shore, and the midrib part of the dabberlocks is still considered pleasant to eat in some districts. Farmers with land near the coast still cut weed from the rocks to feed to cattle and sheep, as well as to fertilise the soil, a practice well known in Wales in the sixteenth century, being recorded in the writings of Owen: 'After spring tides or great rigs of the sea they fetch it in sacks on horse backes, and carie the same, three or four miles, and cast on the lande, which doth very much better the lande for corn and grass.'

As a boy during the early 1940s I helped to collect seaweed, pack the wet stinking fronds into sacks and load them on to a horse-drawn cart. They were then taken to the railway station and disappeared under a haze of steam to the inland farms of Britain striving to feed the nation. Less seaweed is used these days and it is often left to pile up and decay on holiday beaches, a breeding-ground for hordes of flies which then

138

An expanse of Laminaria *at low tide in Robin Hood's Bay, Yorks* (Author)

annoy the visitors. The councils of holiday towns and local farmers could perhaps come to an agreement over the removal and use of these heaps.

It is not only as a direct and indirect source of food that seaweeds have been useful to mankind; they also had considerable industrial value, and indeed still have in parts of the Hebrides and the Orkney Islands. Many species of brown seaweeds were collected, heaped up on the shore, and eventually burned to an ash which was sold as a valuable source of soda and potash used in the making of soap and glass. It was only when alternative and cheaper supplies of the raw materials were found that the kelp industry floundered. In 1820 for example, over 1 million tons were collected annually by the people of the Outer Hebrides and the Orkneys. The decline was halted for a while by the discovery that iodine could also be produced from potash, but chemists found a cheaper alternative and the crofters' livelihood collapsed. The kelp industry has risen yet again with the discovery that alginates from brown seaweeds have many other uses – such as imparting smoothness to jelly and blancmange mixtures, emulsion paints, toothpastes, shaving creams and Turkish delight.

Whatever the fortunes of the seaweed industry, the value of the plants to the animals of the shore remains constant. The zoological zonation is also obvious when the seaweeds that protect them are removed.

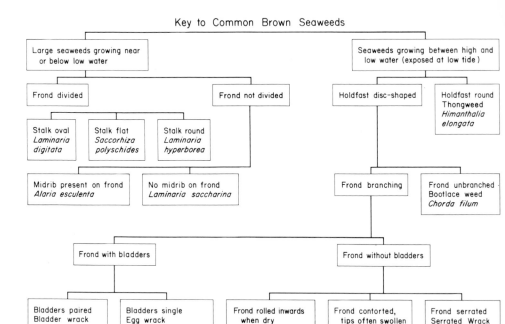

Key to Common Brown Seaweeds

Animal Zonation

By their very nature animals are of course much more mobile than plants, and no attempt at a rigid zone-classification system can work. But the landward area of a rocky shore tends to be dominated by barnacles, which are replaced by periwinkles, the univalves then giving way to bivalve mussels.

The Barnacle Zone

There are several species of barnacle, two of the common ones being the acorn barnacle (*Balanus balanoides*), the commonest of all rocky-shore animals, and the star barnacle (*Chthamalus stellatus*. A casual glance at an encrusted rock suggests that barnacles must be molluscs. It was only in 1833 that J. Vaughan-Thompson, an army doctor and a naturalist, published his researches on acorn barnacles, showing that the larval stages in fact resemble those of prawns and water-fleas; barnacles are crustaceans, the only ones with such a sedentary adult stage. For this reason they are grouped together – as *Cirripedia* (Latin *Cirrus*, a hair), which is a descriptive name, for when the tide is in the barnacles' tight limy plates open and six pairs of featherlike structures emerge to filter out particles of food. These 'cirri' are the equivalent of the legs of more typical crustaceans. The current of water that they draw in also serves a respiratory function.

These sedentary crustaceans have a different system of reproduction from their free-moving relatives: following the usual pattern of sedentary animals, they are hermaphrodite. But they do rely on an interchange of sperm between neighbours, each individual having a long penis for this purpose. The development of the egg takes some sixteen weeks. The larvae then join the plankton before settling down on a rocky shore, or even on the shell of another, perhaps more mobile, species, or on the hull of a ship.

The area in which they settle seems to determine how quickly they develop and also how long they live. Those higher up the beach grow more slowly, as you might expect, and they breed in their second year rather than their first, but they compensate for this late start by surviving for five years instead of three which is the typical lifespan of those nearer the open sea. Where the acorn and the star barnacle occur together, the latter is always higher on the beach. Both flourish best in exposed conditions, but even here they are not free from predators, the most formidable being the dog whelk (*Nucella lapillus*) which wanders up from the periwinkle zone.

Whelk shells vary in colour, but most are white, brown or yellow. It was a small gland in the mantle which made the dog whelk a valuable commodity in Ancient Rome: when exposed to air the gland turned a lovely purple colour and was used to dye the Emperor's toga. The dog whelk can attack the shells of other molluscs and of barnacles by one of two methods: it either bores directly through, or it produces an acid which eats away the carbonates which make up the shells. A specially toughened tongue called the radula is then thrust through the aperture and the flesh of the prey is rasped away. It seems to be the diet which mainly determines the colour of *Nucella lapillus*; if feeding upon barnacles the shell tends to be off-white. Some workers suggest that it is the degree of exposure which is responsible. I subscribe to the former view, but there is no doubt that the degree of exposure does determine the shape of the shell, especially during its early stages of development. During breeding, which takes place during spring, the females. lay clusters of yellow vase-shaped capsules, selecting sheltered rock crevices for the purpose, a habitat which is also favoured by periwinkles.

Periwinkle Zone
The dominant animals of the middle zone of the shore are often the rough periwinkle (*Littorina saxatilis*) and the flat periwinkle (*Littorina littoralis*). The edible species (*Littorina littorea*) may also be present in some numbers up on the splash zone, where the small periwinkle (*Littorina neritoides*) is found. Periwinkles are all herbivores, browsing upon algae. They have separate sexes and internal fertilisation. They can close their shells by means of an operculum, so they can easily

survive desiccation – although direct exposure to sunlight is a different problem altogether. The small periwinkle has several features enabling it to be as much a land dweller as a marine animal: it feeds on lichens, breathes air through a lung-like gill chamber, and adjusts its breeding cycle so that the female releases her capsules, each containing a single egg, into the high spring tides of autumn and winter. The larva lives in the plankton for a while after hatching, and the young adults settle in the barnacle zone before moving their smooth black 6mm ($\frac{1}{4}$in) shell up into the splash zone.

The rough periwinkle thrives in the middle region of the shore and may even on occasion wander as far as the splash zone. The shell is distinguished from other winkles by being deeply grooved and as with the dog whelk there is great variation in colour. The gill structure is somewhat less efficient for 'breathing' atmospheric air than that of the small periwinkle, but is more efficient than that of the flat or common species, a variation that accounts for their relative distribution along the shore. The rough periwinkle breeds throughout the year and is ovoviviparous (producing eggs that hatch inside its body), thus sparing the young the hazards of life in the plankton. The only factor controlling the population is the overcrowding of suitable areas.

The flat periwinkle thrives throughout the zones dominated by bladder wrack and toothed wrack, using the seaweeds both for food and for shelter. It is slightly larger than the rough periwinkle – 1.5cm, or just over $\frac{1}{2}$in – compared to 1.2cm, or just under $\frac{1}{2}$in – and the shells show a greater variation in colour, ranging from white to black through shades of yellow, red and brown. This is the only species whose spawn may be found on the beach, the females sticking gelatinous masses of eggs beneath the wrack fronds; up to a hundred young winkles may develop inside this jelly, using their radula to chew their way out about a month after laying.

The edible winkle at 3.5cm (about 1$\frac{1}{2}$in) is the largest. The apex of the shell is much more pointed than that of the other winkles and the dark red to black colour often shows a distinct darker banding. Unlike the flat periwinkle this species has not managed to break free of the sea: the egg-capsules, produced from February to June and each containing about five eggs, are released into an ebbing tide, hatching into veliger larvae about a week later. These larvae float about in the plankton for a further couple of weeks before settling on the shore.

Although the winkles are the dominant animals, other shells of course occur in the same zone, including the almost triangular toothed (or

Sea wall exposed at low tide, showing the zonation of algae. Rock samphire is growing on top of the wall, at Pennington, Hants (Andrew Cleave/Nature Photographers Ltd)

142

thick) topshell (*Gibbula lineata*) and the painted topshell (*Calliostoma zizyphinum*). These and other species of topshell are also found in the next zone, which is dominated by the common mussel (*Mytilus edulis*). The habitat is often shared with the limpet, although this is also found in the winkle and barnacle zones.

The limpet family is in many ways the most highly adapted of the marine molluscs. The common British species belong to the genus *Patella*: *Patella vulgata*, *Patella depressa* and *Patella aspera*, the last two species being more frequent in the south and south-west. The three are not easy to distinguish by looking at their shells; the experts identify them by the structure of the radula.

Three aspects of the browsing limpet's life are of interest – its almost uncanny homing instinct, its method of attaching itself to the substrate and its way of coping with desiccation. When a limpet is covered with sea water, it leaves its 'home' to browse on the local vegetation; when the tide recedes, it returns to the precise spot it used before. In experiments, a tracing has been made in paint on the rock around the shell; that limpet has left to find food, then settled down again exactly within its circle.

William Wordsworth was another who spent some time studying nature on the coast:

> And should the strongest arm endeavour
> The limpet from its rock to sever,
> 'Tis seen its love support to clasp
> With such tenacity of grasp
> We wonder that such strength should dwell
> In such a small and simple cell.

The animal uses suction to hold its place, but some workers do not think that this alone would be sufficient to resist the full force of the sea, and are looking for an additional mechanism. The contact between the limpet and rock is complete, preventing loss of water through the joint, so there is no danger of desiccation. The limpet can therefore live higher up on the shore than the mussel, which needs more frequent dowsing by the sea.

Mussel Zone
This is often extensive. Each mussel (*Mytilus edulis*) holds its position by means of strong fibres called byssus threads, which are produced by a gland in the foot. The threads somewhat resemble the guy-ropes of a tent and can be loosened to allow the mussel to move a little. Other less common species of mussel may occur, including the horse mussel (*Modiolus modiolus*). The common mussel is not restricted to rocky shores; provided stones or pier supports are available, it will survive

almost anywhere. The shells, reaching a maximum of 10cm (4in), the average size being about half this, are somewhat more asymmetrical than the majority of bivalves, and this is thought to be due to their exposed position on the shore. The mussel's mode of feeding and breathing, however, is fairly typically bivalve: a current of water is drawn over the gills, plankton and oxygen being filtered from it; waste products from the 'kidneys', and carbon dioxide, pass out in a current which is maintained by richly ciliated openings rather than by long siphons. This mode of filter-feeding is bound to pick up any poisonous pollutants, and it is advisable to keep mussels which are to be eaten in a bucket of clean salted water for a day or two to allow such materials to be eliminated by the animals' own body chemistry.

Mussels spawn early in the year, the increasing temperature of spring apparently being the trigger for the release of eggs and sperm. The resulting larvae exist for a while as part of the plankton before settling down for periods of up to seven years in a mussel bed. In the now sadly reduced oyster (*Ostrea edulis*) the byssus-thread system is replaced by a calcareous cement which forms a firmer attachment to the substratum; but both species have a number of formidable predators, including the voracious common starfish (*Asterias rubens*). A typical echinoderm, its whole body is richly supplied with bony scales situated just below the skin – indeed the name echinoderm means spiny skin. When the animal is turned over, a groove can be seen running along each of its five arms, and it is in these grooves that its tube feet are situated; these resemble those described for the heart urchin in Chapter 6. Again we find water-filled canals, but this time the suckers are used for attachment to solid surfaces, and are also adapted for opening bivalve molluscs such as mussels and oysters. Two 'arms' are attached to one valve and three to the other and then a tug- or rather a pull-of-war develops. Eventually the bivalve weakens and the starfish pushes its stomach out of its mouth and into the gap between the valves. It then pumps out digestive juices, and when the breakdown of the bivalve tissues is complete it sucks back the nutritious soup. Some years ago I was working on starfish near Brightlingsea in Essex, and frequently observed this method of feeding, but I also noticed that smaller bivalves were taken directly into the stomach through the mouth and slowly digested in situ.

Large populations of starfish can be a problem to commercial shell fishermen, and their early attempts to control the predator often made matters worse: any starfish they caught were chopped up and thrown back in the sea, for the fishermen did not then know the phenomenal powers of regeneration this animal possesses. It can soon repair wounds and even grow new arms quite quickly.

Asterias rubens is not the only starfish to be found on a rocky beach. Many others may be there, including sunstars (*Solaster papposus*), the

Rockpooling at Flamborough Head, Yorks (English Tourist Board)

spiny starfish (*Marthasterias glacialis*) and the common brittle star (*Ophiothrix fragilis*).

Rock-Pools

A remarkable aspect of life on a rocky shore is the intricate and intimate relationship between seaweeds and the many forms of animal life that live in, on and around their fronds. Once the weeds are lifted the true beauty of the life forms can be seen, greatly adding to the obvious charms of a rock-pool – a lovely marine aquarium, rich in seaweeds, fishes and those delightful 'animal flowers' the sea anemones. There are however many big problems to be overcome by creatures living in these situations. If the pools are stranded after spring tides, then hot weather during the neaps will cause increased salinity – or heavy rains will have the reverse effect. Animals such as the common shrimp, the common prawn, the shore crab and the three-spined stickleback, all described in Chapter 2, will survive well enough in these conditions. Further down the beach the pools will be deeper, be covered more often by the sea and therefore be much more stable in both temperature and salinity. It is here that the anemones are seen at their best.

Sea Anemones

These are members of a very primitive animal phylum, the Coelenterates ('sac-animals'), which also include the mobile jellyfish. The body form of the creatures in this group is very simple, consisting of two layers of cells embedded in a jelly-like material called the mesoglea. Some are mobile, but the so-called polyp types, to which anemones belong, are stuck to rocks – by means of fluid produced by the basal disc. The body opening, serving as both mouth and anus, is surrounded by a varying number of tentacles, which wave about in the water. On these tentacles are batteries of sting cells, each usually made up of an inverted spear-shaped structure set in a bath of poison and with a sort of trigger called the cnidocil. If any animal touches the trigger the cell fires, thus impaling and immobilising the prey; the anemone then feeds by 'licking its fingers'.

The most common species is the beadlet (*Actinia equina*). Although there is some variation in colour the majority are deep red, the positions of the sting cells being marked by purple blotches.

The anemones' feeding method often results in scraps of food being left over and they seem to tolerate the presence of the sea spider (*Pycnogonum littorale*) as it cleans up the mess; this does prove that the anemone can exercise some degree of control over whether or not to fire the sting cells. This type of association is referred to as commensalism – which literally means feeding at the same table.

Some of the anemones are amongst the most beautiful of all marine creatures, especially the multicoloured flower anemone (*Sagartia elegans*) and the daisy anemone (*Cereus pedunculatus*). Sea anemones are most common in the south-west but the snakelocks (*Anemonia sulcata*) occurs all around the coast. It earns its vernacular name from the fact that, unlike other species, it is not able to withdraw its tentacles into its body. I remember finding some splendid specimens in the rich rock-pools at Robin Hood's Bay in North Yorkshire, including the largest and stockiest intertidal species, *Tealia felina*, which the locals call the scaur-cock – scaur being the local term for the rocky outcrops which are so much a feature of this area of the coast. Many of these anemones are more than a match for the free-swimming inhabitants of the pools – the crustaceans in particular, but some of the smaller fish also succumb. Larger fish may be stung but usually survive to fight another day.

Rock-Pool Fish

Rock-pool fish may be permanent residents or visitors stranded by one tide and awaiting the next. The sticklebacks mentioned in Chapter 2 will be found, as well as eels, but more regular inhabitants of rock-pools, often hidden away beneath a rock or fringe of seaweed, are the rocklings, which are close relatives of the cod and typified by prominent barbs projecting from the jaws. The three-bearded rockling (*Motella tricirrata*) has two barbs on the snout and one on the lower jaw; the five-bearded rockling (*Motella mustela*) has four on the upper and one on the lower jaw. Although their body length can be over 30cm (12in), the dark body surface of both species makes them hard to see against the murky background as they wait for their prey. The scales are small and tough, thus preventing damage as the fish slides across rocks, and part of the dorsal fin narrows to a fringe which dovetails into a groove. This is rich in tastebuds, and as rippling movements of the body drive water along the groove, prey is located chemically.

The gobies are another interesting family, of about ten species. Each of these goggle-eyed fish is small and usually lies concealed under the sand. The sand or common goby (*Gobius minutus*) abounds in rock-pools at all levels of the shore and also copes well in estuarine conditions. It is about 5cm (2in) long and is typified by its quick jerking movements before it disappears in a puff of sand. As with the sticklebacks, the males play a prominent part in the survival of the eggs – which are large and pear-shaped. He hunts for a suitable nest site, often beneath the empty shell of a queen scallop, spiny cockle or common mussel, and is then prepared to defend his territory against all comers. Immediately after laying her eggs the female swims off, but the male takes his duties much more seriously and by flapping movements of his fins drives water over the eggs to supply oxygen, a process which he maintains for some two weeks. Other members of this gregarious family include the rock goby (*Gobius paganellus*), which is more common in the south, reaching 20cm (8in) and the ubiquitous spotted goby (*Gobius ruthensparri*), which has deserted the floor of the pool and lives amongst the weeds.

Three species of blenny are also found in pools. Their bodies taper backwards from the broad head with large eyes, and a dorsal fin stretches almost from head to tail. There is the shanny or common blenny (*Blennius pholis*), the well-named butterfish or gunnel (*Centronotus gunnellus*) and the larger viviparous blenny or eel-pout (*Zoarces viviparus*) up to 60cm (24in) long and a tough species which in Britain has a pronounced north-easterly distribution. As its scientific name implies it has a method of copulation resulting in the retention of eggs within the body of the female for some twelve weeks; they are then released in batches of 50 to 350 depending upon the size of the fish. Each young viviparous blenny can be up to 3.7cm (1½in) long at birth and quite able to fend for itself.

In contrast, the common and more widespread butterfish, which breeds from December to March, protects its eggs, both males and females enfolding them with their long, slimy eel-like bodies. After four or five weeks the eggs hatch and the larvae are ebbed out to sea, where they form part of the plankton for some months before returning to the shore. Although these young fish are much more vulnerable than those of the vivaparous blenny they are distributed over a much wider area.

The shanny, like the butterfish and many other shore-dwelling species, has no scales, but its body is protected by a thick layer of soft slime which helps it slide amongst sharp rocks, and also gives protection if the fish gets stranded between tides on a drying beach. The broad tough teeth can crack barnacles and even limpets. The breeding season lasts from April to August, at which point the male assumes a devilish all-black garb with a pair of white lips. This 'uniform' helps him to protect the yellowish eggs which the female secretes in a crack in a rock.

Before leaving the fish of our rock-pools, two more species must be mentioned, if for no better reason than to use their evocative names – father-lashers and cobblers! In fact both species are often called the sea-scorpion. The bullhead or father-lasher (*Cottus scorpius*) and the long-spined sea-scorpion or cobbler (*Cottus bubalis*) both have broad flat heads surrounded by a ruff of spines and are obviously related to the fresh-water bullhead (*Cottus gobio*). They are aggressive predators and the spines are poisonous, especially during the protracted breeding season which lasts from December until May. They can be handled with care, but not without protest from the fish, both species producing loud grunting noises by vibrating their gill covers. Why, one might ask, should it be necessary to handle the spiny beasts at all? If you feel along the region of the lateral line then it is possible to separate the two species; that of *Cottus scorpius* is smooth, while the equivalent area on *Cottus bubalis* is covered by a row of rough scales. Both species can reach a length of 20cm (8in) and with their spines erected can be formidable indeed.

The Sea Urchin

So can the common sea urchin (*Echinus esculentus*), which is more closely related to fish and other vertebrates than might be supposed. The position of echinoderms in animal taxonomy is interesting, for it was from this 'spiny-skinned' phylum that vertebrates, which also have bones under the skin, evolved. Sea urchins have also been important in medical research because their eggs are similar in shape, and in the sequence of their early divisions, to those of human beings.

Although sea urchins are usually found just below the low-water line, they can also occur in rock-pools. The ancient natural historians often take a beating from modern natural scientists, but Aristotle was a good marine biologist even by modern standards, and his knowledge of sea urchins, which were often eaten in his day, was thorough. He knew, for example, that they moved by using their spines and tube feet, and how well they were adapted to their particular niche. 'The urchin has what we could refer to as its head and its mouth down below and a place corresponding to its anus above. For the food on which the creature lives lies down below, consequently the creature has a mouth well adapted for obtaining the food.' Here is the theory of evolution two thousand years before Darwin. Aristotle went on to give details of five sets of jaws and their associated muscles, an efficient mechanism still known today as Aristotle's lantern.

Two Birds of Rocky Shores

Aristotle also knew about seabirds such as the shag – whose scientific name, *Phalacrocorax aristotelis*, acknowledges him. Although shags are often seen standing as if guarding a rocky shore, it is two waders, the purple sandpiper (*Calidris maritima*) and the turnstone (*Arenaria interpres*), which for me are typical of the habitat. The purple sandpiper is just over 20cm (8in), compared to the turnstone's 22.5cm (9in) and has a more slender bill and dull yellow legs; those of the turnstone are bright orange. Neither species breeds in Britain, but J. T. R. Sharrock, in *The Atlas of Breeding Birds of Britain and Ireland*, mentions the possibility that the turnstone may soon attempt to do so. A look at the edition of Yarrell's *British Birds* revised by Saunders in 1885 shows that this possibility has been seriously considered before.

> By the latter part of July young birds make their appearance, but the bulk of the migrants from the north do not arrive until August. On the East coasts of England comparatively few birds remain after the autumn, but on the southern coasts, and especially in the mild climate of the west, many stay throughout the winter. By the middle of May the return migration has begun, and birds in breeding plumage have frequently been observed on our coasts, sometimes in pairs, all through the summer; nevertheless the breeding of this species in the British Islands, although several times suspected, does not appear to be as yet fully proved. On 28th May 1861, a pair rose from a most suitable locality at Lundy Island, and the male unfortunately fell to a hasty shot from the editor's companion.

Once more we see the Victorians' over-hasty use of the gun; it is just as well that Britain is so well endowed with islands, many sufficiently isolated to receive only rare visits from 'editors' companions'. It is to the natural history of Britain's lovely chain of islands that the next chapter is directed.

8

Islands

If once you have slept on an island
You'll never be quite the same.
You may look as you looked the day before,
And go by the same old name,
You may bustle about in street and shop,
You may sit at home and sew,
But you'll see blue water and wheeling gulls,
Wherever your feet may go.

Rachael Field

Anyone who has had an association with any island will understand this poem; and to a naturalist an island can offer the additional bonus of showing evolution in action. One way in which a new species of animals or plants can be formed is by populations becoming geographically isolated. Charles Darwin found that on the Galapagos group the various islands had developed new species differing markedly not only from mainland South America, but also from each other. Intense geological activity had thrust these islands out of the sea, a sort of blank canvas on which a tapestry illustrating evolution has been woven. They are obviously much more remote than any of our British islands and therefore less likely to receive potentially confusing immigrations from the mainland.

St Kilda

The most isolated, and therefore perhaps the most interesting, of all our islands is the St Kilda group, now designated as a nature reserve run by the National Trust for Scotland – although there is an army missile-tracking station on the main island of Hirta. Having visited the island several times I have not felt that the army intrudes; the atmosphere of a naturalists' paradise remains. One has the opportunity to study the St Kilda wren, the graceful gannet, the fascinating fulmar and the unique Soay sheep, not to mention the flora and the archaeological treasures.

The St Kilda Wren
This is the best-documented of the island sub-species, though other

151

St Kilda before the evacuation in 1930 (Margaret Shaw-Campbell)

birds such as dunnocks, song thrushes and even starlings all show minor variations from mainland types. There is weighty evidence to support the theory that the wren family evolved in the Americas and spread across the Atlantic, at a time when the land between St Kilda and the British mainland may have been a series of tree-lined sheltered valleys, ideal for breeding wrens. Then came the melting of ice with the subsequent rising of the sea level. As the climate continued to change and the waters rose, the St Kilda group of islands and smaller rocks were formed from what had originally been the tops of hills. In such exposed conditions larger species and individuals often survive best – as Bergmann's law states – and over the years the St Kilda wrens, hanging on to a precarious existence, tended to become slightly larger than the mainland type. Also their claws and bill have become slightly longer and more powerful, enabling them to extract insects from rock crevices rather than from fissures in tree bark. Isolation from the mainland species has also resulted in the development of a slightly modified song. At one time the St Kilda wren was classified as a separate species, but these days it is only given sub-specific rank, as *Troglodytes troglodytes hirtensis* (the mainland form being *Troglodytes troglodytes troglodytes*). Apart from its interest to collectors during Victorian times, the wren had no intrinsic value to the St Kildan economy, which was based totally upon seabirds until the time of the complete evacuation of the settlement at Village Bay, Hirta, in 1930. The puffin was an important item of food, but it was the breeding gannets and fulmars which kept the St Kildans alive.

The Gannet

A hungry population will eagerly consume any protein available, and the gannet (*Sula bassana*) provided this at all stages in their life history. Their eggs – the gannet lays only one – were eaten in large numbers, either fresh or after being kept for several weeks in barrels. The villagers were not too bothered about the niceties of their meals and were reported not to object to eating addled eggs, remarking that the flavour improved with time.

The birds were eaten when young (being called 'gugas' at this stage) and as adults; in fact gannets from the Bass Rock near Edinburgh were sold too, in local markets, under the name of solan geese. The St Kildans took eggs from Boreray and Stac an Amin and the young were taken from Stac Lee later in the season. This went some way towards preserving a viable breeding population, the St Kildans acting more like bird farmers than wholesale butchers. The difficulties – or, rather, extreme dangers – attendant on each and every journey from Hirta to the smaller offshore islands can only be fully appreciated once you have made the trip yourself in a small boat. Towering about you the huge slabs of rock are awesome, but even worse is the great Atlantic swell, which pushes the boat towards the sharp rocks with irresistible force, only to be sucked back as the wave breaks. The old St Kildan boatmen must have been able to judge the mood of the sea with precision in order to allow their passengers to gain a staggering foothold at the foot of the

Gannet in flight (Author)

This Bass Rock gannet came off worst in a territorial fight and kept its head tucked in for two hours before flying off apparently unharmed. Eye damage is quite common as assailants stab each other with their dagger-like bills (Author)

cliffs. Once landed the men would begin to climb the cliff. The ritualised technique of hunting gannets imposed even greater demands on these brave souls. St Kildan folklore insisted that the climb should be made at night, commando-style. One individual gannet was supposed to stand guard over its sleeping companions; this vigilant sentinel had to be skilfully stalked and put out of action. The Scots historian Martin Martin writing in 1697 gives an interesting account of a gannet hunt: 'If the centinel [sic] be awake at the approach of the creeping fowler, and hears a noise it cries softly "grog-grog", at which the flock move not; but if this centinel see or hear the fowler approaching it cries quickly "bir bir" which would seem to import danger, since immediately after all the tribe take wing leaving the fowler empty on the rock.'

Most of the carnage was therefore perpetrated during the hours of darkness (short enough in these northern latitudes during the summer). The killed birds were often marked on the webbing between the toes, the shape of the notch indicating the slaughterer, then hurled off the cliff to the boats bobbing on the sea below. At the end of a few days of gannet-hunting the men must have been totally exhausted; and once their haul had been counted they would have been glad to get home and doze before a sweet-smelling turf fire, or lie out on the grassy slopes soaking up the heat of the summer sun. Martin Martin suggests that 22,600 gannets were taken annually, but this seems to have been far too high a figure; more reliable estimates suggest about 2,000 young birds.

These unfortunate gugas were not sacrificed in vain, for the St Kildans had many and various uses for them. The thick-walled stomachs were removed and the oil extracted from the birds was stored in them; both the oil and the feathers were used as items of barter with traders visiting the islands. In the early days these visitors would be few, although the islanders did owe allegiance to MacLean of MacLean whose officers came annually to collect the rent – paid in ornithological currency. Even the long dagger bills of the gannets were used – as staples to secure thatching materials to the roofs of their dwellings. The islanders made good use of other seabirds too, but the gannet remained the main quarry for many years until superseded by the fulmar petrel.

The Fulmar

By the year 1758 the whole St Kildan economy had changed; the gannet currency had been replaced by the fulmar plan. The people may have noticed that the fulmar (*Fulmarus glacialis*) bred on Hirta just behind their Village Bay settlement, and that a difficult boat journey was a waste of energy; but if things were this simple, they would have realised the possibilities long before the middle of the eighteenth century. A better reason lies in the increase in the fulmar's population. Until 1878 St Kilda had Britain's only breeding colony. Since this date the species has spread rapidly around the coastline of Britain; and the trend is continuing to such an extent that some breeding is now being attempted inland. It is quite probable that after centuries of exploitation, St Kilda's gannet stocks were becoming depleted while the fulmar was beginning this very rapid population explosion still with us today. There is no totally convincing explanation for it. One theory is that the scraps plentifully discarded by the expanding whaling and fishing industries served to keep pelagic species such as the fulmar alive during periods of natural food shortages and therefore more survived to breed. The fulmar is in any case a long-lived bird, often surviving for upwards of twenty years. The switch from gannet to fulmar was a perfectly natural progression, reflecting the ecological climate of the time.

The annual number of fulmars killed seems to have remained surprisingly constant at between 100 and 130 birds for each inhabitant of St Kilda. When eaten fresh, the bird was said to be tough, oily and with a taste somewhat resembling beef. Salting-down the bodies does

Nesting fulmars (Author)

not seem to have developed until fairly recent times, and the birds were plucked clean of feathers, split down the middle and stored in special storage chambers called cleitans. Fulmars had one great value surpassing any possessed by the gannet; they produce a rather sticky evil-smelling oil, which both young and adults spit out, often with deadly accuracy, at their enemies; each individual can produce up to one-third of a pint (200cc) and this was the main basis of the St Kildan economy for many years. If the mineral-oil industry had not replaced this bird-oil, the islands might have had a flourishing population today. The fowlers were lowered over the edges of the cliffs, captured the birds with a noose on the end of a long stick, pulled each bird towards them, broke its neck with one deft movement, then upended it and squeezed the oil into a container – still made from the stomach of a gannet. This biological oil-well is situated in a part of the gut called the proventriculus. All members of the petrel family have it, but only the fulmar has learned to use it as a weapon!

The value of the fulmar was obvious by the time Kenneth Macauly wrote his *History of St Kilda* in 1764. He reports an islander as saying: 'Can the world exhibit a more valuable commodity? The fulmar furnishes oil for the lamp, down for the bed, the most salubrious food and the most efficacious ointment for healing wounds. Deprive us of the fulmar and St Kilda is no more.'

So much then for its economic importance. Its natural history is also interesting. The evil-smelling oil ejected by disturbed birds was known to the people of Iceland before the tenth century as the 'foul maa', and as 'maa' means gull, this translates as the stinking gull. To the modern taxonomist the fulmar is not a gull, but it certainly has a superficial resemblance to them. It is only the 'tube nose' so typical of the petrels that makes the distinction easy, although in flight the fulmar holds its wings stiff and straight, not bent at the 'elbow' as they always are in gulls. Another vernacular name is 'mallimoke', deriving from the Dutch and meaning 'stupid gull': the bird earned this by its tendency to sit tight on its single egg even in the face of extreme provocation. This must have helped the St Kildans, used to stalking wary gannets at dead of night.

The fulmar's one egg (occasionally two) is laid in late May and both sexes share the incubation, which lasts for about fifty-five days, taking it in turns to sit for about four days at a time. They look after the chick until it fledges, approximately sixty days after hatching. During much of this period the chick is a chubby bundle of white down.

The fulmar is colonial and the breeding ledges are occupied as early as November at some sites, as late as February at others. By April the colony is full of sound and fury but signifying a great deal, as territories are sorted out and laying begins, the whole ritualised sequence of behaviour ensuring that all the birds lay their egg at about the same time. The last birds have usually departed by mid-September; during the next few months the fulmars wander far and wide, feeding upon the fat of the sea. The young birds are in no hurry and do not usually return to their breeding ledges until their sixth year.

Thus the St Kildan group had plenty of food (of a sort) to offer its human inhabitants due to the teeming bird populations – which still make the often-sickmaking journey across the treacherous stretch of sea from the mainland worthwhile for the naturalist.

St Kilda also once had its own sub-species of house mouse (*Mus musculus muralis*). This became extinct soon after the settlement was abandoned.

Soay Sheep

But the primitive Soay sheep (*domestica*), still survive here. They are often said to be of Scandinavian origin and tradition credits their introduction to a Viking named Calum, but some archaeologists are convinced that they are associated with prehistoric (probably neolithic) settlements. The species was described by the historian Boece as long

157

ago as 1527. 'Beyond Hirta is another uninhabited island [he means Soay]. In it are certain wild beasts not very different from sheep. The hair is long and tallie (dull) neither like the wool of sheep nor goat.'

Soay sheep were kept by the St Kildans who also kept the normal breed which has its origins in southern Europe. In the Soays, both sexes are horned, the ram more resplendently. The sheep occur in two colour phases, light brown animals outnumbering near-black ones by about three to one; the hair of both is much more like that of a goat than normal sheep's wool. In 1932, some two years after the evacuation, about 100 sheep were transported from Soay to Hirta and the present population now hovers between 600 and 1,900. They have been the subject of intensive scientific study financed by the Nature Conservancy ever since this time.

The Small Isles

Although the St Kilda group in general and Hirta in particular are amongst the best-documented of the Hebridean islands, some of the others have their own ecological treasures – none more so than the island of Rhum (see Chapter 1), with its experimental herd of red deer. Rhum, however, was not the first west-coast island to serve as an open-air laboratory for the study of Britain's largest land animal; it was on the lovely island of Jura that Henry Evans conducted his intensive studies. Jura, its so-called paps rising like breasts from the body of enfolding sea, is beautiful at any time, but when viewed across the sound from Loch Sween, especially at sunset, it takes on an almost magical quality. Along with its neighbour Islay, it also possesses an unusual type of stoat (*Mustela erminea*) which shows minor variations in the head shape as well as having small ears. Whether it deserves to be classified as a sub-species, with the title *Mustela erminea racinae*, has not yet been decided.

With Eigg, Muck and Canna, Rhum forms the group known as the Small Isles. Of the many islands on which I have slept I would choose to be stranded on Canna, for it was there that in the course of one memorable night I listened to the unique sound of Manx shearwaters blending with the monotonous grating of corncrakes, and at the end of the extravaganza watched a pair of otters playing in the water. Until 1981 Canna was under the benevolent ownership of John Lorne Campbell, an eminent naturalist and Gaelic scholar who for over forty years took pains to conserve the wildlife and traditional way of life of the island. It now belongs to the National Trust for Scotland, so should not change too much. No harmful chemicals have been used on the land, and the dozen farm workers (the whole population is but eighteen souls) cut their crops late enough and with sufficient leisure to avoid the nest of

Otter in the Hebrides (Bill Wilkinson)

the corncrake (or land rail) and leave it to breed in peace. On the mainland, in areas of high-intensity farming, this bird's demise has been largely due to today's need to force crops fast and cut them with machines. That night in quiet, gentle Canna, low cloud and Hebridean rain did not dampen my enthusiasm as, curled up on a coil of rope that had drifted in from the sea and wrapped conveniently round a rock, I heard the eerie high-pitched calls of those Manx shearwaters returning unerringly in the darkness to their burrows on the grassy slopes. The Bretons once called these birds 'the souls of the damned', and their noise could well play on the nerves of the superstitious. Bat-like systems of navigation are still being investigated, but echo-location seems to be the most likely method of finding the nest site. The magical quality of the shearwaters' calls, and especially the swishing of their wings as they hurtled past, made the June night seem even shorter; all too soon the morning sun lifted the mist like smoke from a peat fire, and dawn spread a blush from the east. Below me on a rock that pair of otters were making short work of what had once been a large fish, and once

159

breakfast was over they played happily together, their high-pitched whickerings carrying on the still air for some distance before echoing around the rocky caverns.

It was a thrill for an English naturalist to see otters in their natural home and we must hope that protection has been given to them in England and Wales in time to save them; many of us have been profoundly disappointed that the law does not extend to Scotland. Presumably they will get no help until they are already doomed to disappear even from their traditional stronghold, Gavin Maxwell's Western Isles.

Special Birds and Insects

If such enjoyment can come with one night on an island, how much deeper must have been the feelings of Ronald Lockley when he spent some years on his beloved island of Skokholm off the coast of what is now Dyfed, Wales, where in 1933 he set up the first bird observatory – and wrote detailed biographies of the puffin and the Manx shearwater, and of course *The Private Life of the Rabbit*. Wales is rich in these small grassy islands; Skomer, south of St Brides Bay, is renowned for the variety of its wild flowers as well as for its own sub-species of vole (*Clethrionomys glareolus skomerensis*), which is bulkier than the mainland type. The 8 hectare (20 acre) island of Grassholm has a thriving colony of gannets, but it is Skokholm that is the best documented, through Lockley's work. Its flat-topped dark red cliffs, once the lookout posts of hordes of Vikings, are now manned by a much friendlier group, wardens from the West Wales Naturalists' Trust who maintain the observatory.

Moving south and sailing eleven miles out to sea off the north Devon coast at Hartland, we find an island just over three miles long by half a mile wide, with impressive granite cliffs approaching heights of 130m (400ft). Lundy is the Norse word for puffin and though there have been human settlements here since Neolithic times the island has traditionally belonged to the sea parrot. The puffin (*Fratercula arctica*) is the most attractive of the auks, and its huge multicoloured bill is unique among British birds; its coloured layers are moulted, at the same time as the plumage. On Lundy's cliffs grows the 'Lundy cabbage' (*Rhynchosinapis wrightii*), found nowhere else in the world.

So far we have looked mainly at our island-based vertebrates, but evolutionary forces are likely to work even more quickly upon isolated communities of less mobile insects and rooted plants. Many of the Hebridean islands have their own special forms of butterflies, including grayling (*Hipparchia semele*), small heath (*Coenonympha pamphilus*) and meadow brown (*Maniola jurtina*), but whether these varieties should be upgraded to the rank of sub-species is open to debate. We are probably watching evolution in action, and this is why it is important that accurate and regular surveys are made of our island faunas. Migrant forms are likely to settle on islands before spreading to the mainland, or in some cases they may remain only on the island. The Glanville fritillary (*Melitaea cinxia*), for example, is confined to the Channel Islands and the Isle of Wight; the Isle of Man has its own species of grasshopper (*Stenobothrus stigmaticus*) and the Channel Islands are the only British site for the blue-winged grasshopper (*Oedipoda caerulescens*). Havergate Island is rightly famous for its breeding avocets, but it should not be forgotten that here is found a unique spider, *Praestigia duffeyi*, only named in 1953. The peculiar invertebrates of our islands could well be the subject of a volume on their own; many islands have their own particular gem. But when it comes to a consideration of island flowers, the Scillies must take first place.

Islands and Flowers

Are the Scillies the most isolated part of Britain, as some travel writers would have us believe? Despite the remote situation of this tangle of almost thirty islands and countless rocks, the warming waters of the Gulf Stream have enabled a couple of thousand people to thrive for thousands of years among a most varied fauna and flora. Banana trees and tropical palms flourish in the magnificent botanical gardens at Tresco. Spring flowers are ready for market as early as February and the sight of the wild flowers is worth the agonies of the nearly always choppy sea crossing in the flat-bottomed vessels which are needed to dock in the shallow, rock-strewn harbours. Seaweeds coat these rocks and kelp-burning was once as important here as in the Orkneys and the Western Isles. Among the host of flowering plants found on the Scillies (and often on the Channel Islands also) are the dwarf pansy (*Viola kitaibeliana*), orange birdsfoot (*Ornithopus pinnatus*), Cornish mallow (*Lavatera cretica*) and shore dock (*Rumex rupestris*); while a tiny fern, early adder's tongue (*Ophioglossum lusitanicum*) grows here and nowhere else in the United Kingdom except the Channel Isles.

Travelling further north, we find growing on Walney Island a sub-species of the bloody cranesbill (*Geranium sanguineum*) growing on the sand dunes. These delicate pink blooms are found wild only on Walney, which is so close to Barrow-in-Furness that it is hardly an island at all and has been bridged for many years. This area was 'annexed' by Cumbria following the 1974 changes in county boundaries, but of course the plant retains its scientific name of *Geranium sanguineum* var *Lancastriensis*. Standing on the shores of Walney it is possible to see the

Isle of Man on a clear day. Here too are some particular species, including the Isle of Man cabbage (*Rhynchosinapis monensis*) which was first described by Ray on the island in 1660. But since this time it has been found growing along the western coast of Britain – I have found it at Walney, Roanhead, Eskmeals, Ravenglass and Maryport. It is interesting that the Manx shearwater was first named from a now extinct colony in the Calf of Man. A plant which grows on the Isle of Man however, is the dense-flowered orchid (*Neottia intacta*); although it also grows in southern Ireland it is typically a Mediterranean species.

On some islands it is not so much the rarity of a flower but the superstition which surrounds it which is of interest. This certainly applies to the sea bindweed (*Calystegia soldanella*), which grows in many places but is rare in the Western Isles, apart from on one beach on the fascinating island of Eriskay. Although a tiny island administered from South Uist, Eriskay is very well known in consequence of its traditional love-lilt and because it was the setting for the novel and film *Whisky Galore*. There were very few residents there at the time of Bonnie Prince Charlie's landing in 1745, when some seeds of the sea bindweed which had somehow got into his pockets in France – it is said – were discarded on the white shell beach and took root. It also grows at one other spot in the Hebrides, at Vatersay near Barra, but no tradition explains why it should be there!

The 310 hectare (766 acre) Handa Island off the coast of Tarbet in north-west Scotland is now an established RSPB reserve with some of the most impressive cliffs in Britain, including its huge Stack. There is also an extensive graveyard which tradition tells us was established on Handa to prevent the corpses being unearthed by hungry wolves, which only occurred on the mainland.

Further north still, a long boat trip or short flight will take us to the once remote Orkneys and Shetlands. Things there have changed dramatically in the last ten years with the discovery and exploitation of the oilfields. Fortunately the ecology of these remote spots has been well documented, as has that of the Farnes, Wight, Man or any other more accessible and heavily populated areas. As the next chapter will seek to demonstrate, industry and wildlife can, and in many cases must, learn to live together for the mutual benefit of both – a sort of survival symbiosis. This way our island fauna and flora will not only survive but continue to evolve – and provide stimulating work for the scientists of the future!

Annet, Isles of Scilly, with thrift dominating the foreground (P. Wakely/Nature Conservancy Council)

9
Coastal Wildlife and Industry

We all need energy. Coal burning pollutes the atmosphere, oil spills destroy wildlife and can be aesthetically disastrous, gas terminals swamp the landscape and atomic radiation could sterilise half the population and kill the rest; but we cannot do without energy. Compromise must be the only sensible road. The Friends of the Earth organisation and the Atomic Energy Authority have one thing in common – neither would welcome a radiation leakage. This is what should be receiving publicity, rather than the polarised arguments. Oil companies and naturalists too have an important area of agreement. Both hate oil spills, one because – at the very least – they cost money and bring unpopularity, the other because they destroy wildlife. The naturalists who do the complaining drive from one protest meeting to another, filling their vehicles with fuel on the way; again, compromise is the only answer. There should be stringent laws to protect the environment, but industry cannot close down. We could support the introduction of an 'anti-pollution' levy compelling firms, whether state-owned or not, to pay a tax, the money being used to fund relevant ecological research. Many companies give freely at the moment, but we must ensure that what is given is neither too little nor too late and is used to best advantage.

The Chemical Industry

To most of us the thought of a chemical complex conjures up pictures of a sterile and biologically hostile environment with pulsating plant belching pollutants into the atmosphere. We are given reasons to support this view – for instance the *Sunday Times* of 25 October 1981 carried a story by Simon Freeman which suggested that Canvey Island was a potential disaster area to the human population of some 30,000 living in the fifteen square miles amongst oil and chemical installations. At the time of writing the full impact of an unpublished government report on the island has not been felt, but General Sir Richard Ward has gone on record as saying that there was enough faulty equipment to make an accident distinctly possible. A leakage could release a cloud of explosive propane gas six miles wide, putting as many as 12,000 human lives at risk.

164

A naturalist reading this would imagine that wildlife would already be absent from such areas. But the important, if geographically limited, work of Gordon Youdale shows otherwise. Youdale, who works as an electrician at the Severnside Chemical Plant, has published lists of species found in and around the works. His bird list is long and impressive, including a night heron (*Nycticorax nycticorax*), which was found sheltering in the compression building of a nitric-acid plant. The management sensibly encouraged these studies and allowed nestboxes to be sited around the complex. Thirty-seven species have been found breeding in and around Severnside works, including cuckoo, grasshopper warbler, whitethroat, spotted flycatcher, redstart, treecreeper, great spotted woodpecker and long-tailed tit. Kestrels also breed on an old disused plant once used in the manufacture of ethylene glycol.

Mammals too have found suitable habitats on the site; foxes, badgers, weasels, water voles, rabbits, and hares have all been seen, and doubtless there are other smaller and less conspicuous mammals such as shrews and rodents. These must find the warm pipes useful areas during long cold winter nights. So do roosting flocks of starlings and pied wagtails. In summer many flowers thrive amongst the industrial 'plants', their seeds attracting such species as linnets, goldfinches and reed buntings, especially in the damper areas of the complex.

Very few works are fortunate enough to have such competent naturalists on the staff, but a similar report could, I am sure, be made from many of them. This is yet another example of nature's resilience. But even this is stretched beyond breaking-point around some of our heavily industrialised estuaries, where we ourselves may be threatened too. The wildlife is functioning as a pollution indicator: what affects birds and animals today may well affect us tomorrow. Deaths of birds due to chemical pollution often go unnoticed, except when they are on such a massive scale that the attention of the media is caught. During the autumn of 1979 the effects of massive pollution were noted on the north shore of the Mersey estuary, just west of Hale. After the histrionics had abated the event was succinctly covered in the British Trust for Ornithology's *News*, published in December 1979. The deaths recorded during the first two months of the outbreak are shown (including over 1,000 dunlin). The editorial noted

The Mersey is heavily industrialised and there are many potential sources of pollution. It is possible that the deaths are a result of lead deposited in the estuarine silt many years ago and only recently stirred up by dredging operations. Some mud samples have contained very high levels of lead indeed. The inorganic lead in the mud is not, in itself, an immediate danger to the birds. However many species of mud dwelling invertebrates, which are horrifyingly efficient concentrators of lead, form the main food of many of the estuarine birds; this is probably how they are being poisoned.

The report also goes on to mention the discovery of eleven dead rats, and one hedgehog which probably perished after eating contaminated corpses.

Anyone reading this account out of context might gain the impression that the Mersey estuary is dying, but the true position is the reverse. Twenty years ago the area was so polluted that very few birds were around to be poisoned. Stricter laws and more enlightened management (it would be naive to suggest that the two are unconnected) have reduced the quantity of dangerous effluents entering the river, and the improvement has been almost as dramatic as that of the Thames, so well documented by Wheeler, Harrison and others. Species which have returned to the Mersey include the pintail, which dabbles in the shallows for its food, the shelduck feeding upon *Hydrobia* (see Chapter 7), and many species of wader. All that the Mersey-estuary deaths prove is that birds are present but vulnerable. Obviously naturalists must strive for many further improvements, and for more concerned attitudes, but we must take care not to be too pessimistic either. ICI are blamed for polluting the environment, yet they have co-ordinated research into problems which would be impossible to solve if we were dealing with thousands of independent units. ICI's Brixham laboratory, founded by the paint division in 1948 to develop and test paints resistant to sea water, has become world-famous in its much wider environmental role. Here scientists not only work to limit ill-effects from ICI's own products but frequently act as watchdogs for other industries which lack such facilities. The value of this work to our wildlife cannot be overestimated. Studies of currents around our coasts, and estimates of how quickly pollutants spread, can have far-reaching implications.

Gas and Oil

Many other major industries are aware of the pressures and their obligations, none more so than British Gas, who face a classic 'Catch 22' situation. The country needs gas and this means a pipeline, which must be brought ashore somewhere; there is bound to be controversy wherever these and their associated complexes and compressor stations are sited. The main worry of the coastal naturalist is that a suitable place for a pipeline landfall will be one of the softer, more easily eroded, dune systems, a fact also well known to those responsible for these delicate negotiations; a fairly lengthy quote from *Gas Plants and People*, the one-hundredth communication of 'The Institution of Gas Engineers' illustrates this:

> The route of the pipeline from the offshore field to the coast will generally take the shortest possible route to a 'soft rock' landfall where the

pipeline can be brought ashore easily. Although it is technically possible to lay the pipeline over a 'hard rock' coastal area, the costs of so doing will be excessive and there may be serious operational problems in protecting the pipeline from damage. Soft rock coastlines which may be favourable for the landfall comprise two types: first, areas of sand dune systems, as at Theddlethorpe and St. Fergus, or low cliffs in consolidated sands and/or clays as at Bacton and Easington. Development may have an impact on either type of landfall; it is potentially greater on the sand dune areas.

Areas of dune development may appear to the layman to be of low agricultural value and may appear to be derelict. However, many of these areas are of very high scientific value, and in some cases unique and of worldwide interest. The plants and animals which have become adapted to this very specialised environment are of particular importance due to their adaptation. Their protection is of increased importance because such areas of active sand dune are becoming restricted due to the demands of development, e.g. sand extraction for building purposes and the pressures of recreational usage. It is ironic that the areas most suitable for pipeline landfalls are also those most susceptible to disturbance.

Sand dunes are particularly dynamic and easily eroded unless careful measures are taken to control wind-blow. The effects are not specific to the dunes alone as sand encroachment on adjacent land can be serious, causing not only loss of agricultural land but in certain, albeit infrequent, cases the engulfment of villages. This has occurred in the past such as at Culbin on the Moray Firth and at the sands of Forvie, near Newburgh between Aberdeen and Peterhead. The method of formation of sand dune systems indicates the vital importance of careful management of these sites. Whilst on most beaches there is a seasonal variation in the volume of sand in the foredune area, (i.e. that closest to the sea) due to the erosion of the front of the dune during storms and the accretion of sand by wind-blow from the beach; the whole system may be thus balanced, and in such a system, the dunes will be stable. Nonetheless, there is much evidence to show that the initial formation of some dune systems may have resulted from a single large storm or a series of such storms, as seen in the areas of Newburgh Warren, Anglesey in 1331 and the Lock of Strathbeg immediately north of St. Fergus in about 1720. Just as a large storm can form a dune system, so any dune system can be seriously disrupted by large-scale storm events, and if such disruption were to occur while or immediately after a pipeline was laid through them, the effects on these dunes could be very serious. As mentioned earlier, the sand, particularly when dry, is extremely easy to erode; indeed, this ease of movement is one of the attractions of making the landfall in such an area. But, since pipe-laying takes place in the summer when the sand is at its driest and most mobile, erosion could occur on the sides of the pipeline trench during the lengthy period of preparation, pipelaying and back filling, causing damage to extend beyond the immediate vicinity of the pipeline easement. The method used at both Theddlethorpe and St. Fergus has been for the clearance of the dunes on either side of the easement and the storage of sand behind the dunes to enable the pipeline trench to be sheet piled prior to the pulling ashore of the pipeline. When pipelaying is complete, the sheet piling is withdrawn and the sand is replaced and recontoured. This method means that an area considerably greater than the pipeline easement is affected due to the angle of repose of the sand. Whilst the practice of contractors to date has been to leave these temporary sand faces unvegetated, the use of bitumen spraying or mulching to control sand blow has been found to be beneficial.

The effects of these pipelaying operations on sand dune hydrology are not clear. The dunes are extremely porous and the drainage of water is virtually unimpeded since pore space may equal 30 per cent by volume. The removal of large sections of the dunes during pipeline construction may, therefore, affect the 'water-table' on either side of the easement for some considerable distance. The effects of this disruption are poorly understood at present. Certainly, the plants in the higher sections of the dune, such as marram grass (*Ammophila arenaria*) are specialised to the environment to such an extent that water requirements may be met solely by intermittent rainwater and pendular water (i.e. dew etc). The problem is more complex in the lower areas towards the back of the dunes where the lower-lying dune slack areas involving a much wider variety of plant species may be seriously affected. This could be of great significance since non-indigenous species may inadvertently become established if careful management measures are not taken during reinstatement. The problem was highlighted at both Theddlethorpe and St. Fergus by the proximity of areas of very high scientific interest which are scheduled as Nature Reserves to the north of both sites.

The normal methods of reinstatement of areas which have been affected by pipeline landfalls are similar to those which have been adopted in other sand dune areas, disrupted either by excessive recreational use, or excessive grazing by rabbits or by disturbance during war-time use as training grounds. Fences may be used to promote sand dune accretion in areas which have been subject to 'blow-out', the fence acting in the same manner as the snow fences seen adjacent to main roads. Once sand has begun to accumulate or, in the case of reinstatement, when work has been finished on the recontoured pipeline easement, the area is hand-planted with marram grass. This is usually carried out in regular patterns as at Theddlethorpe, where the interposition of sea buckthorn (*Hippophae rhamnoides*) has been used to promote further accretion of sand and prevent erosion of newly established areas. The growth of sea buckthorn takes some time to establish, and the easement is distinguishable by the lack of mature growth compared with adjacent areas.

These methods are extremely time-consuming and expensive, and require the prevention of damage by rabbit grazing. In many cases, re-planting is required in successive years if the treatment is to be fully effective, since the failure rate of planting is often high. The use of bitumen or mulch spraying and more recently, the application of treated sewage sludge has been used in some areas to stabilize the surface of the sand. These methods also provide a stable growing medium, including nutrients, which promote the growth of a wider range of species than does hand-planting, and promotes a more complete cover than that of marram or sea lyme grass. Recent work at Liverpool University on these techniques suggests that nutrients are required to promote rapid growth of plants. As yet, this method has not been used on the Corporation's sites, but may be adopted if considered suitable.

In many respects, the treatment of the pipeline landfall through sand dunes is merely a specialised form of pipeline reinstatement, involving a particularly difficult type of working area. There are other areas and types of environment which may be equally susceptible to disturbance by pipeline operations which pose equally difficult problems.

To some degree at least, the oil companies face a similar problem to the gasmen: the siting of their pipes will always result in controversy. In addition, oil terminals, tankers and drilling stations are all liable accidentally to spew out the odd few thousand gallons of fuel in most inconvenient places. Nothing is better designed to polarise an already difficult situation. Naturalists demand an alternative source of fuel and the oilmen counteract this by giving scholarships to naturalists, funding films and underwriting the production of splendid books on the wonders of natural history, forming birdwatching societies based on oil rigs and generally showing that they not only understand wildlife, but actually worry about its preservation almost as much as they do about shareholders' profits!

In 1979 the oil companies agreed to form the North Sea Bird Club and associated with it are the Scottish Ornithological Club, the Nature Conservancy Council, British Petroleum, Shell, Chevron, Phillips, BNCC, Conoco, Mobil and Occidental in consultation with Aberdeen University. Realising the advantages of oil platforms as ornithological observation posts, the companies have provided the rigs with binoculars, reference books and record forms. It is hoped that their daily records will filter through to the unversity, where they will be stored on computer tape. Details of bird movements could be vital, since in the event of 'serious' oil spills it would be handy to know if any 'regular' flocks were in the area.

To this end it would be useful to have details of sea currents flowing though the area. During June 1981 I was beachcombing with a group of students and friends in the area around Loch Noydart to the north of Oban, when we found a plastic card released by C-CORE. This is the Center for Cold Ocean Resources Engineering operated by Memorial University of Newfoundland. The card was returned to them and their reply told us:

> The card you found was released at Flemish Pass about 200 miles North East of St. Pauls Newfoundland (49°18'N 49°37'W) on 4th August 1979 as part of an ocean current study. The information gained from the cards will be used to predict the drift path of possible oil spills.

The fact that oil spilled north of Newfoundland could well end up, unless previously dispersed, on a Scottish beach underlines that oil pollution must be tackled on a global basis; accidental oil spills are possible anywhere and at any time. Research and back-up capital are needed to find the best method of dealing with it. Not that this is the only line to take: there should be massive fines for the owners of tankers which deliberately clean out their oil tanks at sea. The large numbers of birds killed in a single large oil spill are nowhere near the numbers killed by many smaller slicks which do not make headline news.

The RSPB have been actively involved in collating information as part of their Beached Bird Survey and in 1979 published *Oil Pollution and Birds*. An article in their magazine *Birds* gives us cause for optimism but not complacency.

For the first time in four years the number of birds known to have been oiled in major pollution incidents has decreased. In 1979/80 fewer birds were affected than in either of the previous two years, the first year showing a decrease since 1974/5. Ten incidents, each involving more than 50 birds, occurred between July 1979 and June 1980. Over 6,280 casualties were recorded, slightly more than half the number (11,847 birds) recorded in 1978/9. In Shetland, where serious pollution incidents during 1978/9 led to stricter enforcement of pollution control measures, only one incident was recorded, involving 79 little auks, amongst other species.

The largest kill last winter occurred in south-west England in December, when nearly 3,000 birds were washed ashore between St Ives, Cornwall, and Woolacombe, North Devon. Attempts to rehabilitate over 600 birds, mainly guillemots, at the RSPCA's centre at Little Creech, Somerset, were unsuccessful because of the difficulty of removing all traces of the particularly waxy fuel oil. Examination of a small number of these guillemots suggested that they were from southern populations (*albionis*) and four of the six auks reported wearing rings came from the colony on Great Saltee Island, Co Wexford. The incident was the largest kill to have occurred in south-west England since 7,851 birds were recorded oiled in Cornwall after the 'Torrey Canyon' went aground in March 1967.

On 19 March another incident occurred on the vulnerable north-east coast of England, this time affecting more than 2,000 birds. A series of oil slicks was observed between the Farne Islands and Tynemouth during a Department of Trade aerial survey requested by the Nature Conservancy Council, but a second flight the following day in poorer visibility failed to locate any oil. No further action was taken to search for or disperse the oil, but live oiled birds continued to come ashore for the next five days. Discussions were subsequently held between the DoT and the NCC and the RSPB to improve response to future incidents in north-east England.

Large bodies such as the RSPB, RSPCA, British Trust for Ornithology and the British Naturalists' Association have a great part to play in liaising with oil companies; but what part, if any, can smaller bodies or even individuals play? The work of Eric Cowell should serve as an inspiration. He was responsible for the setting up of the Oil Pollution Research Unit at Milford Haven, and his lead has been followed by others such as Jenny Baker and Brian Dicks. The unit have carried out invaluable researches into pollution of the sea in general and by oil spills in particular. They have been able to compare the sea around Milford Haven before and after the construction of the giant oil terminal, as well as study the effect of the developing petrochemical complexes on Southampton Water. More recently the unit have benefited from grants made by the Institute of Petroleum, the Leverhulme Trust and the World Wildlife Fund and have made studies of the effect of oil operations on the seabed at Ekofisk, Forties, Auk, Brent, Magnet, Maureen Burton and Beatrice fields. They have hit upon the sensible idea of using sedentary organisms as indicators, since they cannot move away from pollution and must therefore feel its full effect. Much work has yet to be done in this area, but it must be done: as oil supplies begin to run down towards the end of the century, 'difficult' fields will have to be tapped and this must inevitably mean greater risks of spills. By this time an alternative form of energy must be found. Harnessing the energy from the tide's waves has been suggested; this too must pose some threat to wildlife if and when it becomes financially and physically feasible. Nuclear power is perhaps the best alternative source, but this is even more contentious than oil – and that is saying something!

Nuclear Power

Conservationists do malign the nuclear industry – the loudest complaints often coming from those who know least. Electricity is the most versatile fuel in use today, but it is not a primary fuel and has to depend on either hydroelectric schemes or thermal power plants, which all rely upon converting water into steam, which then drives the electric

UKAEA research power stations, CEGB and SSEB nuclear power stations, and BNFL works in England, Scotland and Wales (United Kingdom Atomic Energy Authority)

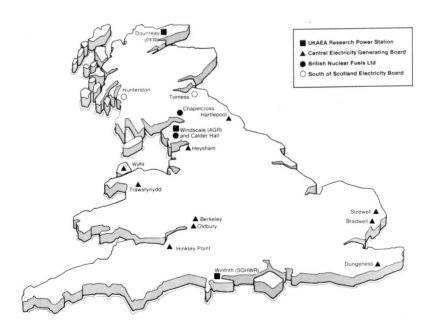

turbines. Coal, oil, gas and nuclear fuel are all used to heat water.

A nuclear power station is comparatively cheap to run. But only about 3 per cent (in 1981) of our electricity is produced from atomic stations: this must rise dramatically as fossil-fuel reserves run down, which means – the doom-and-gloom brigade tell us – that we shall be blown to kingdom-come or perish from massive doses of radioactivity. Their facts are lacking; radiation is a natural phenomenon and 80 per cent of the doses to which we are exposed in the United Kingdom comes from cosmic rays from space, the rocks of the earth itself, especially granite, and even our own bodies. 'Artificial' sources of radiation are fall-out from nuclear testing, television screens, radioactive tracing and X-ray techniques used in hospitals. Nuclear power stations at present account for only one-thousandth of our annual dosage. Sitting in front of the television is a little bit more dangerous than man-made radioactivity and a flight in an aircraft cruising at 40,000 feet is much more dangerous!

Atomic power stations are built around the coast as the water used to cool the plant can be discharged into the sea; many people fear that this will adversely affect the genetics not only of the fish but also of anyone foolish enough to eat them. Again this is exaggerated. It has even been proved that the hot water discharged raises the nearby sea-temperature sufficiently to enable plaice to develop from eggs to marketable size in half the normal time. So – can we allow the industry to get on with its own business? No, since there is a slim chance that dangerous leakages could occur, and conservationists must keep up intelligent pressure to ensure that safety levels are maintained. All nuclear power stations have a series of safety barriers built into their design to prevent substantial leaks. In 1979, due to a series of mishaps, a power station on Three Mile Island at Harrisburg in the United States went 'out of control' and confirmed the worst fears of the pessimists; but it is sometimes forgotten that no employee, let alone any member of the public, was injured.

If Three Mile Island is the first in the firing-line in the States, then Windscale is the target in Britain. It is to Windscale that the spent fuel from other plants is brought after an initial cooling-down period. Yet many of us who are ardent conservationists find little to complain about, since each flask which rumbles its way along the west-coast rail route weighs some 50 tons and is designed to withstand temperatures of 800°C, immersion in 15m (50ft) of water, and if necessary the shock of a severe crash.

Some estimates suggest that radioactive elements in some of the organisms in Morecambe Bay have risen dramatically between 1970 and 1980. There is as yet no evidence to prove that these levels will eventually be ecologically disastrous, but objective monitoring must be continued and even extended despite the cost. Those who love wildlife would be better employed in trying to influence industry chiefs on the positioning of future plants, rather than whether any should be built at all. This is where the naturalists' knowledge of rare or particularly vulnerable flora and fauna can play a vital role.

The Holiday Industry

The holiday complexes which have mushroomed around our coastline present a difficult poser. Which most harms wildlife – temporary disruption of a relatively small area by the construction of a vital energy factory, or a spread of caravans across a dune system, their occupants' feet trampling over often unique habitat week after week throughout the summer? As much care should be taken in siting these summer cities as with any chemical, gas, oil or nuclear complex. Even the sewage outfall from such areas could be not only aesthetically disastrous but a problem for marine organisms. In order to break down sewage, the bacteria concerned require plentiful supplies of oxygen; and when large quantities of sewage are involved, the oxygen in the water may be too depleted to allow normal respiration, so that many of the natural organisms perish.

This problem can be observed around most of our seaside resorts, but EEC regulations are already showing signs of bringing about an improvement. We can be fairly optimistic that the 1992 British beach will be cleaner than its 1982 equivalent, provided naturalists keep up their barrage of constructive suggestions.

Gazetteer
101 Special Places to See

Each of these places has contributed something to the making of this book. So have many others, and the Gazetteer could well be longer than the rest of the book; so I have restricted it to an arbitrary number, remaining very conscious that any other marine naturalist could draw up an equally impressive and totally different list.

The numbers are those used on the map on page 176. The places mentioned are not in any order of merit.

1 Abbotsbury Swannery, Dorset
In summer there is a unique colony of breeding mute swans, established in the fourteenth century. Signposted off the A35. In winter there is good birdwatching in the Chesil Beach area.

2 Aberlady Bay, Lothian, Scotland
A nature reserve off the A198 between Edinburgh (16 miles) and North Berwick (9 miles). Public access and car parking. Rich in mudflats and saltings. A seawatch here is always rewarding, especially in autumn and winter, and long-tailed ducks, scaup and eider may be seen, with the occasional rarity such as white-billed divers. The thrift zone of the saltmarsh is at its best in June.

3 Ailsa Craig, Strathclyde, Scotland
An important island, with the 1,000ft cliffs supporting a large gannetry. About 11 miles from Girvan. Permits to land obtainable from the Information Office, Town Hall, Girvan. Interesting tours around the island can be arranged with the boatmen of Brodick, Isle of Arran.

4 Ainsdale and Freshfield, Lancashire/Merseyside
This Southport area has an attraction for birdwatchers, and is also a dune system rich in plants, including the large-flowered evening primrose, and a breeding area in the slacks for natterjack toads. Access to this and to the nearby red-squirrel reserve is free (a small fee for parking). The richness of the area is retained despite its popularity with picnickers.

5 Aldingham and Bardsey, Cumbria

Follow the A590 to Ulverston and thence via the coast road to Barrow. These small but impressive shingle beaches overlook Morecambe Bay. In summer they attract botanists and lepidopterists. In winter the offshore mudflats of the bay have high wader counts.

6 Arbroath Cliffs, Tayside, Scotland

From the large car park, take a pleasant walk along the red sandstone cliffs, with their many interesting formations and bore-holes. The area is botanically and entomologically rich and also has some breeding sea-birds, rock doves and house martins.

7 Bamburgh Sands and the Farnes, Northumberland

A magnificent dune system with rich growths of lady's bedstraw, marram, rest harrow, bird's-foot trefoil, etc. The area leads to Sea-houses and beyond it the Farnes. Excellent seawatches can be had at all seasons, with seals and killer whales as well as the obvious birds. Huge breeding colonies. Boats to the Farnes start from Seahouses. The islands are owned by the National Trust and non-members will be charged a landing fee.

8 Bardsey Island, Wales

Situated 2 miles south-west of the attractive Lleyn peninsula. Accommodation is available at the bird observatory, which has a resident warden. Day visitors are conveyed from Aberdaron (landing fee). All aspects of coastal natural history may be studied here.

9 Bass Rock, Lothian, Scotland

A circular island, rich in seabirds but especially gannets. Reached by boat from North Berwick: contact the boatman, Freddie Marr, 24 Victoria Road, North Berwick. Other bird islands in the region include Fidra, The Lamb, Eyebroughty and Craigleith. There is an unusual type of tree mallow and varied animal life among the rock-pools.

10 Beachy Head, Sussex

Near Eastbourne, can be reached via the A259. First-rate observation point for seabird movements, and the site of a ringing station operated by the Sussex Ornithological Society. The general naturalist will find interesting flowers, especially in July.

11 Bempton Cliffs, Yorkshire

Reached from Bridlington via the B1255. A very impressive cliff system, botanically and ornithologically rich. Vast colonies of kitti-wakes are here, and Britain's only mainland gannetry. Now wardened

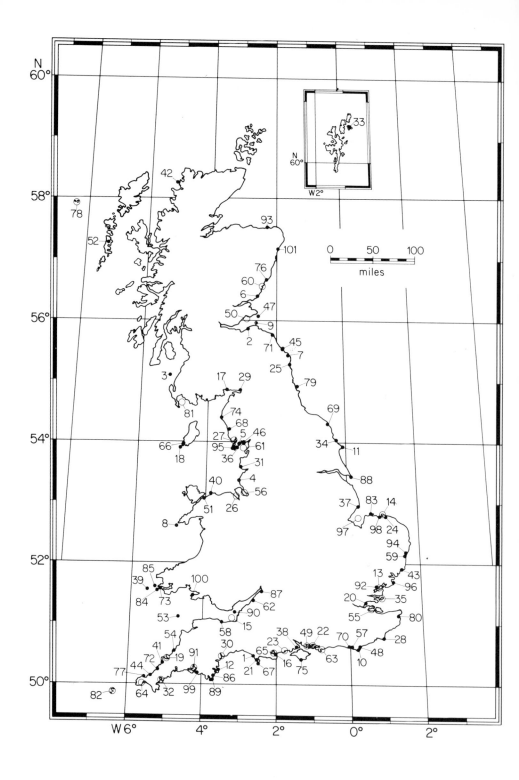

in summer by the RSPB. The chalk-cliff system ends at Flamborough
Head. To go straight to the Head and lighthouse follow the B1259.

12 Berry Head, Brixham, Devon
This area, about 1 mile east of Brixham, can often be crowded with
tourists in summer. If visited early in the morning good views can be
had of nesting auks, kittiwakes and fulmars.

13 Blackwater Estuary, Essex
Best reached via the B1026 to Goldhanger and beyond this a lane leads
to the sea wall. The toughened birdwatcher will find accommodation at
the Bradwell Bird Observatory, c/o A. B. Old, Bata Hotel, East
Tilbury, Essex. A very important estuary for Brent geese, wigeon,
shelduck and other wildfowl, as well as autumn waders such as
whimbrel and godwits.

14 Blakeney Point Complex, Norfolk
Fed by the A149 road, this area is rightly famous in the ornithologist's
world, but there is also much for the botanist and entomologist to see.
The National Trust maintains a 1,300 acre reserve consisting of a super
dune system plus a large colony of common terns. It also holds Britain's
largest colony of little terns. The harbour is a favourite spot for waders
and a large flock of Lapland buntings often frequents the area.

15 Bridgwater Bay, Somerset
A National Nature Reserve reached from Bridgwater via the A38 or
A39. Access is free except on to Stert Island. Very varied habitat,
including saltmarsh, shingle spits and over 2,400 hectares (6,000 acres)
of mudflats, which serve as moulting grounds for shelduck as well as
roosting and feeding areas for wildfowl and waders. Includes the Parrett
estuary and carries high bird counts at all times of year.

16 Brownsea Island, Dorset
This island of over 500 acres is the largest in Poole Harbour and is leased
by the National Trust to the Dorset Naturalists' Trust. Private boats
may not land but boat trips are run from Sandbanks Ferry and Poole
Quay. There is a landing fee and guided tours begin at the church on
several days a week. Red squirrels may be watched, and the island is
rich in many forms of wildlife.

17 Caerlaverock, Dumfries and Galloway, Scotland
The area is rightly famous for the Caerlaverock National Nature
Reserve which has large areas of mature saltmarsh and mudflats. The
B725 and B724 are the roads to take; the Wildfowl Trust reserve at

177

Eastpark Farm is reached on the B725. The whole area is famous for the increasing wintering flocks of barnacle and greylag geese. Intending visitors should contact: The Warden, The Wildfowl Trust, Eastpark Farm, Caerlaverock, Dumfriesshire D91 4RS (Glencaple 200).

18 Calf of Man, Isle of Man
Lies off the west coast of the Isle of Man. The splendid bird observatory has accommodation. Birds are ringed here as part of the BTO's study of migration. Details from The Secretary, Manx Museum and National Trust, Douglas, Isle of Man. Resident choughs. Warblers pour over and on to the Calf, including occasional barred, icterine, melodious and subalpine. Lapland and snow buntings, woodchat, shrike and red-breasted flycatcher have been recorded.

19 Camel Estuary, Cornwall
Good views can be had from the B3314 road off the A39. The area is excellent for winter wildfowl while on autumn passage – little stints and curlew sandpipers are often seen.

20 Canvey Point and Island, Essex
The depression felt on reading parts of Chapter 9 may be dispelled somewhat by following the A13 to Great Tarpots and proceeding via Benfleet to Canvey Point, where grey plover, ringed plover, terns, skuas and wildfowl can all be found in impressive numbers – depending, of course, on the season and state of the tide.

21 Chesil Beach, Dorset
Well-known to all students of shingle beaches (see Chapter 4), this area is a good place for a winter seawatch, when long-tailed ducks, mergansers and divers may be seen. Wintering short-eared owls also glide over the area, and on one occasion I watched seven separate birds hunting in a force 8 gale, their flight control being remarkable in the conditions.

22 Chichester Harbour, Sussex
A first-rate birdwatching area in autumn and winter. Black-necked and Slavonian grebes often recorded, as well as Brent geese, eiders, mergansers, little stints, greenshanks and purple sandpipers.

23 Christchurch Harbour, Hampshire
Although not large, the habitat is varied and includes saltmarsh and mudflats; it often attracts interesting waders and passerines.

Guillemots and kittiwakes on the Farne Islands (Owen Newman/Nature Photographers Ltd)

24 Cley, Norfolk

The A149 road runs through Cley and Salthouse Marshes. To the student of coastal botany the area is a delight, and it is also thought by the experts to be the best birdwatching area in Britain, ideally sited and provisioned to attract continental migrants and vagrants.

25 Cullernose Point, Northumberland

From Alnwick take the B1340 to Hocketwell and then to Craster. Excellent seawatches can be had from the point to Dunstanburgh, and there are cliffs and a rocky shore full of fascinating pools. Seaweeds and interesting invertebrates, as well as fishes, abound.

26 Dee Estuary and Hilbre Island, Cheshire

Divides England from Wales. There are ideal spots on both sides to watch wildfowl and waders. Red Rocks on the English side is a good vantage point, and Hilbre Island and its smaller offshore rocks are amongst the best wader-watching areas anywhere in Britain. Take care to check tide times before walking across. The main island – from which seals may be watched – is visited only by permit, obtained from Hoylake Urban District Council, Hoylake, Wirral, Cheshire.

27 Duddon Estuary, Cumbria

Sandwiched between Millom and Roanhead. Reached via the A595 which skirts the estuary. The splendidly rich dune systems have breeding natterjack toads, and little terns. Good wader and wildfowl counts.

28 Dungeness, Kent

Dungeness is one of the most-studied shingle beaches and is of great interest to the botanist. The presence of a nuclear power station (see Chapter 9) brings one down to earth but the area is still an ornithological treasure at any season. Visitors may stay at the bird observatory which sleeps about ten, visitors doing their own chores. Details from The Warden, Dungeness Bird Observatory, Dungeness, Kent. There is also an RSPB reserve close by. For permits apply to the Warden at Boulderwall Farmhouse.

29 Eskmeals Dunes, Cumbria

Run by the Cumbria Naturalists' Trust. No permit is needed but if more than ten people plan to visit the area together they should notify the Trust's Administration Officer at Rydal Road, Ambleside (tel 2476, mornings only). The reserve is a peninsula formed at the junction of the River Esk, just off the A595. The reserve has sand dune and saltmarsh, a colony of black-headed gulls and is particularly attractive to botanists. Cinnabar moths and fritillary butterflies are found, and roe deer occasionally lie up in the long grass.

30 Exe Estuary, Devon
Take the A379 from Exeter and turn left at the sign for Powderham, or further south look for Starcross. There are over 1,000 acres of the Exe Estuary bird sanctuary to be enjoyed. The area is good at all times but especially in winter, when wildfowl, waders and grebes abound. Dawlish Warren is also worth a visit, especially for the botanist.

31 Fairhaven to St Anne's, Lancashire
Despite its proximity to the popular beaches of Blackpool, this is a splendid area of sandflats, attractive to waders throughout the year. Sanderlings are plentiful in May and early June and snow buntings often occur in winter. The marine lake is attractive to wildfowl in winter.

32 Fal Estuary, Cornwall
The area is a complex of small muddy estuaries, good for waders and coastal plants. The most interesting areas are Devoran Creek (off the A39) and the Truro river in the area around Malpass. Having once had the good luck to ground a hired boat in this area, I spent the rest of the day surrounded by greenshanks, spotted redshanks, common redshanks and a host of dunlin.

33 Fetlar, Shetland
An RSPB reserve famous for the snowy owls which bred in 1967. This event tends to overshadow the general excellence of the island for naturalists. Details of accommodation may be had from the RSPB, The Lodge, Sandy, Beds, or from the Warden, Bealance Bothy, Fetlar via Lerwick, Shetland.

34 Filey Brigg, Yorkshire
A mass of rock-pools full of fascinating coastal vegetation and animal life. The mile-long finger-shaped brigg also affords good birdwatching and is easily reached from the town, which lies 7 miles south of Scarborough. See also Bempton Cliffs.

35 Foulness, Essex
Reached from Southend via the A13, turning left after a couple of miles or so along the B1017 to Great Wakering. Used by the Ministry of Defence, so there are many human restrictions. Brent-geese flocks can often exceed 5,000 birds but many other wildfowl – especially wigeon – are also present, feeding on the expanses of eel grass. The casual

181

birdwatcher is not welcome in many places, but there are good views to be had from the road without trespassing.

36 Foulney Island, Cumbria

Off the A5087 coast road between Barrow and Ulverston; situated close to Walney Island the area is the site of an impressive ternery, and the shingle beach has botanical merit for here grows the rather rare oyster plant. The island is wardened in summer and access restricted to avoid disturbing the terns. A good place to watch winter wildfowl and waders.

37 Gibraltar Point, Lincolnshire

An excellent birdwatching area provided with a residential observatory. The reserve is just off the A52. Details are available from the Field Station Warden, Gibraltar Point, Skegness, Lincs (tel Skegness 2677). Good ringing statistics and species lists. All naturalists are well catered for; over 250 moths and 15 species of butterfly occur on the reserve. The dune system is well developed and typical.

38 The Gins, Hampshire

Access to this area is by permit by the Hampshire and Isle of Wight Naturalists' Trust. It is reached via the A35 and the B3056 to Beaulieu. The B3054 then leads to Bucklers Hard and Needs Oar Point. Ornithologically rich, and famous as the first British breeding site of the Mediterranean gull.

39 Grassholm, Wales

Those wishing to visit the splendid gannetry (22 acres), some 10 miles off the Pembrokeshire coast, should write to the RSPB representative at 18 High Street, Newtown, Montgomeryshire SY16V 1AA. Be prepared to be disappointed because landing is not easy.

40 Great Orme, Wales

A good car park at the end of Llandudno esplanade, or reached by the Great Orme railway. Lovely cliff walks, interesting flowers and breeding seabirds. Best place on mainland Britain for observing choughs. A good spot for seawatchers in autumn.

41 Gull Rocks, Holywell, Cornwall

A good place to watch auks. Take the B3075 from Newquay and after 3 miles look out for a right turn to Cubert and Holywell. The rocks lie off Penhale Point, which is itself a good place to see and photograph coastal plants and scenery.

Eider nesting among tree mallow on Bass Rock (Author)

42 Handa Island, Highland, Scotland

An uninhabited island owned by the RSPB, having many and varied seabird colonies. Also of great interest to the botanist. Reached by boat from Tarbet, which is on the A894 north-west of Scourie. Details of permit from the RSPB, The Lodge, Sandy, Beds.

43 Havergate Island, Suffolk

An RSPB reserve with limited visiting by arrangement (The Lodge, Sandy, Beds). The boat leaves from Orford Quay. Breeding avocets are the main attraction but the shingle spit at Orford Ness is a major botanical attraction.

44 Hell's Mouth, Cornwall

This lovely coastal walk is owned by the National Trust and is some 5 miles long, stretching from Portreath to Godrevy Point. The best access point is from Hell's Mouth itself, just off the B3301.

45 Holy Island, Lindisfarne

Turn off the A1. Sand dunes, sandflats, grass verges, sheltered spots all contribute to making this tidal island a sanctuary for wildlife. Naturalists wishing to stay on Holy Island will find a welcome at Castle View, Holy Island, Berwick-upon-Tweed (tel 0298 272). Lindisfarne and Budle Bay constitute a National Nature Reserve.

46 Humphrey Head, Cartmel, Cumbria

Reached off the A590 just to the west of Cartmel. A botanically rich limestone outcrop into Morecambe Bay. Excellent place to seawatch in winter when waders and wildfowl, especially shelduck, gather in numbers.

47 Isle of May, Fife, Scotland

Reached by arrangement with boatmen from Anstruther or Crail. Visitors are allowed to stay at the Bird Observatory (maximum six). Write to the Bookings Secretary, c/o The Nature Conservancy in Edinburgh. The island is famous for birds and the general naturalist, too, will find much to study.

48 Langney Point, Sussex

Reached via the A259 and B2191. A perfect spot to study a shingle beach in summer and birds in all seasons. There are many houses and even more fishermen, but the area is still rich in natural history.

49 Langstone Harbour, Hampshire

A most valuable reserve of saltmarshes and intertidal mud. Dunlins can number almost 20,000 and wildfowl counts are high. Many interesting species occur on passage, including whimbrel and sandpipers. Greenshank and spotted redshank are often recorded.

50 Largo Bay, Fife, Scotland
Off the A915. The area is interesting in winter for purple sandpipers and scoter, while in summer pochard may breed. Little gulls and velvet scoters have also been noted. There are also rich carpets of dune flowers.

51 Lavan Sands, Wales
Reached via the A55 between Bangor and Llanfairfechan. Splendid sands but some saltmarsh. Rich flora and insect life as well as autumn and winter wildfowl and waders.

52 Loch Druidibeg, Outer Hebrides
A National Nature Reserve of over 4,000 acres. Permits from the Warden, Stilligarry, Lochboisdale, South Uist. Excellent for divers and also botanically interesting. Also fifty-plus breeding pairs of greylag geese.

53 Lundy Island, Devon
Access to the island, 11 miles north of Hartland Point, is best obtained by becoming a member of the Lundy Field Society, which allows you to stay on the island. Seabird colonies including puffins, but also botanically interesting. Enquiries should be directed to the Accommodation Officer, c/o 4 Taw View, Bishop's Tawton, Barnstaple.

54 Lye Rock, Cornwall
Reached by travelling northwards along the B3263 from Tintagel. The rock is famous for its auks, and particularly as the site of the largest puffin colony in Cornwall.

55 Medway Estuary, Kent
This rich area can be reached via the M2 and A2 to Upchurch and then to the small village of Ham Green. The sea wall is a good vantage point but there are plenty of paths skirting the area, which is 8 miles long and over 5 wide, full of oozing mud and banked by rich saltmarshes. A very important area for wintering wildfowl and for waders on autumn passage.

56 Mersey Estuary, Liverpool
The Mersey is not so polluted these days and large numbers of wildfowl including Bewick's swans are found in winter; short-eared owls also winter here. In spring and autumn ruff and golden plover occur in some

numbers. There are extensive areas of saltmarsh of interest to botanists. The best access point is via the A5032 road to Ellesmere Port. Permits can be obtained from the Manchester Ship Canal Company, 2 King Street, Manchester 3. It should be noted that the Frodsham Wildfowlers' Club shoot over part of the area during the season.

57 Midrips and Wicks, Sussex
From Rye follow the A259. The area is a beach of high shingle with sheltered pools behind. Shingle plants abound and the shelter provided often allows the birdwatcher a rare sighting. Snow buntings and many species of wildfowl are regular visitors.

58 Minehead Beach, Somerset
Very varied habitat, including shingle, sand and mudflats. Sand dunes well developed. Ideal for those who wish to see the subjects of the chapters in this book in one small area. It can also be visited from Dunster – car-park fee in summer.

59 Minsmere, Suffolk
A 1,500 acre RSPB reserve, 2 miles south of Dunwich. Details available from the RSPB. A rich and varied habitat, its real potential often overshadowed by the excitement of seeing breeding avocets.

60 Montrose Basin, Tayside, Scotland
Large flocks of waders in winter and a moulting flock of mute swans in summer; I noticed a pair of summering whooper swans during 1981. An interesting foreshore and saltmarsh system. A Scottish Wildfowl Trust Reserve of almost 2,000 acres, but being enclosed it is vulnerable to oil pollution.

61 Morecambe Bay, Lancashire/Cumbria
The area is huge, but is easily watched since the A5105 follows the coastline. There are several points of access, including the RSPB reserve centred on Hest Bank at one end, and Jenny Brown's Point, Silverdale, at the other. Leighton Moss, a breeding area for both the bittern and the otter, also belongs to the RSPB. The wader counts prove this to be one of the best areas in Europe. There are limestone outcrops, areas of sand, saltmarsh and Britain's largest area of mudflats, which ensure something of interest to all naturalists.

62 New Passage, Gloucestershire
Leave M5 via exit 17. Follow to East Compton and then via B4055 to

Bempton Cliffs, Humberside, now an RSPB reserve and home for thousands of kittiwakes, guillemots, puffins and an expanding colony of gannets (P. Wakely/Nature Conservancy Council)

the New Passage Hotel. The area is rich in saltmarshes and has a substantial area of spartina grass. A variety of wader species are usually around.

63 Pagham Harbour, Sussex
Reached from Chichester on the B2145 and B2166. The area has been a nature reserve since 1964. Pagham is a must for the Sussex naturalist.

64 Penzance Harbour, Cornwall
Once the summer tourists have left, this seasonally booming harbour plays host to many visiting birds, including assorted grebes, great northern divers, purple sandpipers, eiders, velvet scoters. It is always worth a visit. As on the Scilly Isles, rarities are likely to turn up during autumn and winter.

65 Poole Harbour, Dorset
Although a popular tourist resort and moderately busy port, the harbour does still, especially in the north-eastern corner, provide a haven for a host of birds, particularly in autumn and winter. Species of particular note include scaup, smew, black-necked grebes, Slavonian grebes and a wide variety of waders. *See also* Brownsea Island.

66 Port Erin, Isle of Man
Excellent bays and rock-pools. A splendid marine aquarium and research centre is run by the Manx government and the University of Liverpool.

67 Portland Bill, Dorset
The Centre is open from 1 March to 31 October and accommodation is booked via the Warden, Portland Bill Observatory and Field Centre, Old Lower Light, Portland, Dorset. As at many observatories the experts have produced an impressive rarities list: Portland has its Bonelli's subalpine, aquatic, Dartford, yellow-browed and icterine warblers, amongst others, to add to the wildfowl, waders and shear-waters which make this one of the blue-riband observatories.

68 Ravenglass, Cumbria
Situated just off the A595. Permits required from the County Estate Surveyor, Arroyo Block, The Castle, Carlisle CA3 8XF (tel 0228-23456). Impressive colony of black-headed gulls, also common, Arctic, roseate, Sandwich and little terns. Natterjack toads, adders and common lizard are also found. The dunes are botanically very rich and in the slacks are helleborines and sundews.

188

69 Robin Hood's Bay, Yorkshire

Situated between Whitby and Scarborough, the rocky beach is the perfect marine laboratory for the student, used as such by Leeds University until 1981 when it unfortunately had to close.

70 Rye Harbour, Sussex

Follow the A259 south of Rye, cross a canal and reach the area via a series of factories. Large areas of shingle and a rich bird habitat, because the shingle has been excavated to produce a number of pits. A nature reserve with access by permit.

71 St Abb's Head, Borders, Scotland

Sandstone cliffs situated some 12 miles to the north of Berwick-upon-Tweed. Access is via the A1107 and B6438. Seabirds and house martins breed here and the botany is interesting, as is the complex folding of the ancient rocks, found all the way to Eyemouth.

72 St Agnes Head, Cornwall

Reached from Redruth via the A30 and B3277. A lovely cliff-top walk takes you to the seabird colonies. There is also a treat here for the botanist and for those who fancy a close-up view of lizards, slow-worms and the adder.

73 St Ann's Head, Wales

This bird-rich area should not be missed, and nor should the nearby Dale Fort Field Centre, close to rich rock-pools. Details of the courses there can be obtained from the warden, and they are well worth the money.

74 St Bees Head, Cumbria

The red sandstone cliffs 2 miles south of Whitehaven are now an RSPB reserve (no permit needed). They support many breeding seabirds and provide the only English site for the black guillemot. There are considerable equinoctial bird movements, including gannets, shearwaters, often ravens and occasionally choughs. In summer the plant life is impressive.

75 St Catherine's Point, Isle of Wight, Hampshire

This, the most southerly point of the IOW, is an excellent place to watch migrants on sea passage, especially in October.

76 St Cyrus, Grampians, Scotland

Close to Montrose and off the A92, St Cyrus is a National Nature Reserve (parking can be difficult in summer), which has wonderful cliff walks to delight the botanist and entomologist. Rock doves and house martins are here found breeding in their natural habitat, as are fulmars and stonechats. An ancient method of salmon fishing, 'stake netting', is still practised on the sandy shore. Well-developed sand dunes are also worth study.

77 St Ives Island, Cornwall
A very pleasant cliff walk, and the ornithologist may see spectacular sea passages – rarities such as Sabine's gull, Balearic shearwaters, Leach's and storm petrels.

78 St Kilda, Outer Hebrides
Access is difficult but once transport is arranged is not restricted. The Mecca of British ornithologists. Write for details to the Scottish National Trust, 5 Charlotte Square, Edinburgh 2. St Kilda has our largest gannetry and large numbers of fulmars and puffins.

79 St Mary's Island, Northumberland
Less well known than Holy Island, St Mary's is also reached by causeway; it lies about 2 miles north of Whitley Bay just off the A193. Good for birdwatching at all times, especially in autumn.

80 Sandwich Bay, Kent
The flora of the bay is of great interest, including masses of rest harrow and sea holly. Sea rocket and sea bindweed are found on the dunes and sea aster and two species of sea lavender on the saltings. Wild asparagus and the lizard orchid also grow near here. There is an important bird observatory and applications to stay should be directed to the Secretary, No 2 Old Downs Farm, Sandwich Bay, Kent CT13 9PF. Pegwell Bay is also worth a visit.

81 Scar Rocks and Luce Bay, Dumfries and Galloway, Scotland
Reached via A746 and A750, Scar Rocks have nesting gulls, and auks, kittiwakes, shags and cormorants breed. The regular seabird passage ensures a good seawatch at all seasons. The sands of Luce and Burrow Head are interesting botanically.

82 Scilly Isles, off Cornwall
This cluster of islands reached from Penzance by rough ship or smooth air lie almost 30 miles off Land's End. Warmed by the waters of the Gulf Stream but also battered by the Atlantic, this is the place to find

The rare clustered bell-flower at St Cyrus, NE Scotland (Author)

botanists studying exotic flowers and ornithologists 'twitching' as they observe rarities driven in by the winds. All naturalists interested in coastal wildlife should make a 'Scilly pilgrimage' at least once.

83 Scolt Head Island, Norfolk

An 1,800 acre island: a National Nature Reserve, an ideal breeding area for terns and a winter refuge for wildfowl. Reached by boat, or on foot at low tide (be careful!), from Brancaster which is on the A149.

84 Skokholm, Wales

Site of a famous bird observatory. Details of visiting available from West Wales Naturalists' Trust, 4 Victoria Place, Haverfordwest.

85 Skomer, Wales

A splendid naturalists' island reached in the season by boat from Martins Haven. Members of the West Wales Naturalists' Trust may land free while other visitors pay a fee. A good area for shearwaters, puffins and storm petrels in summer.

86 Slapton Ley, Devon

A magnificent area of coast and fresh-water lagoon which guarantees excellent natural history in all seasons. A field centre run by the Field Studies Council offers courses in natural history from February to November. Details from the Warden, Slapton Ley Field Centre, Slapton, Kingsbridge, Devon TQ7 2QP. Tel (0548) 580466.

87 Slimbridge New Grounds, Gloucestershire

Home of the Wildfowl Trust formed by Sir Peter Scott in 1946. Reached via the A38 south of Cambridge. Impressive collection of captive wildfowl, plus wild visitors especially Bewick's swans and white-fronted geese. The Severn estuary area has great expanses of marshland, a perfect breeding area for yellow wagtail, lapwing, redshank, reed and sedge warblers and many others.

88 Spurn Head, North Humberside

Cheap accommodation provided by courtesy of the Yorkshire Naturalists' Trust. Write to Spurn Bird Observatory, Kilnsea via Patrington, Hull, North Humberside. Extensive sand dunes and mudflats as well as saltmarsh. Follow the A1033 from Hull and then the B1445. There is an admission fee to get out to Spurn Head. You will not be alone, for Spurn is a magnet to birds and birdwatchers alike.

89 Start Point, Devon

The most southerly point of Devon, with a lighthouse, so the area is excellent for passage migrants, especially those which fly at night.

90 Steep Holm, Somerset

An interesting limestone island of 47 acres lying 5 miles west of Weston-super-Mare. Twelve species of seabird breed here and important ringing work is done. If you are a fanatic and would like to stay overnight details can be obtained from the Secretary, Gull Research Station, 64 Standish Avenue, Patchway, Bristol.

91 Tamar Estuary, Devon

The Tamar is a complex system, the Devon/Cornwall boundary, reaching the sea at Plymouth. There are plenty of wildfowl in winter and also numbers of waders, including avocets, turnstones and black-tailed godwits. There are many points of access.

92 Tollesbury, Essex

This often underrated area is reached from Kelvedon via the A12 and then the B1023 to Tollesbury. There is parking along the sea wall. Impressive saltmarshes support most of the plants described in Chapter 3, and in winter sea ducks are much in evidence. There is a heronry, and Great Cob Island is a breeding area for terns and black-headed gulls.

93 Troup Head, Grampian, Scotland

Reached by travelling east from Macduff by way of Gardenstown along the B9123. The cliff system has nesting auks including the black guillemot and 8,000 common guillemots. Also important for wintering waders.

94 Walberswick, Suffolk

A National Nature Reserve reached via the A12, B387 and B1387. There are dunes, brackish pools and mudflats. Botanically rich and ornithologically interesting. Nightjars, bitterns, bearded tits, shore larks, whimbrels, hen harriers and short-eared owls recorded according to season.

95 Walney Island, Cumbria

The dune system is rich in viper's bugloss, henbane and a unique variety of bloody cranesbill. This is the most southerly breeding area for eiders and has a mixed breeding colony of lesser black-backed and herring gulls. Interesting sea passages in winter, spring and autumn. Cottage accommodation available by writing to the Warden, South Walney Nature Reserve (Cumbria Naturalists' Trust), Barrow-in-Furness, Cumbria.

96 Walton on the Naze, Essex
Reached from Frinton-on-Sea via the B1336. Car park near the cliff edge. Impressive saltmarshes and at Stone Point excellent winter sea-watching is assured. Goldeneye, scoter, merganser, shelduck, eider, grey plover, snow bunting and twite are regularly recorded.

97 The Wash, Lincolnshire
The Wash is a wonderful site for the general naturalist, and especially the ornithologist. Many areas can be reached via the A52, A17 and A149. Friskney, Wrangle, Boston Point, Holbeach, the Nene Outfall, Snettisham and Heacham will all repay a winter or autumn visit.

98 Wells-next-the-Sea, Norfolk
If ever a road was built for birdwatchers it must surely be the coastal A149. 1,000-plus Brent geese winter here, and a free-access National Nature Reserve rich in pines provides good cover for immigrant passerines. There are various points off the A149 which are full of goodies for the coastal botanist.

99 Wembury, Devon
This charming area on the eastern end of Plymouth Sound needs a little care when visited for the first time. Leave Plymouth on the A379 and make for a car park at Wembury Point. The large area of rock-pools is a living laboratory for the marine naturalist. The ornithologist should also keep an eye open in autumn for buzzards, divers and the delightful little firecrest.

100 Whiteford Burrows, Wales
Reached from Swansea via the A4118, B4396 and B4296. Owned by the National Trust, this is an extensive area of splendid sand dunes.

101 Ythan Estuary, Grampian, Scotland
About 15 miles north of Aberdeen, this magnificent area includes Newburgy and Forvie Sands; dune systems, saltmarshes, mudflats can all be studied, and seabirds, waders and wildfowl are all present throughout the year. A moulting area for shelducks and eiders. An oil terminal at nearby Cruden Bay worries naturalists as a potential menace.

Bibliography

General

Budker, P. *Whales and Whaling* Harrap (1958)

Campbell, A. C. *The Hamlyn Guide to the Seashore and Shallow Seas of Britain and Europe* Hamlyn (1976)

Campbell, B. *Birds of Coast and Sea* OUP (1977)

Carson, Rachel *The Sea Around Us* Staples Press (1951)

Chinery, M. *A Field Guide to the Insects of Britain and Northern Europe* Collins (1973)

Clapham, A. R., etc *Excursion Flora of the British Isles* CUP (1959)

Countryside Commission *A Conservation Policy for Coasts of High-quality Scenery* HMSO (1970)

Countryside Commission *The Planning of the Coastline* HMSO (1970)

Cramp, S., etc *The Sea Birds of Britain and Ireland* Collins (1974)

Darlington, A. *Natural History Atlas of Great Britain* Warne (1969)

Dawson, K. *Marsh and Mudflat* Country Life (1931)

Durman, R. (ed) *Bird Observatories in Britain and Ireland* Poyser (1976)

Eales, N. B. *The Littoral Fauna of Great Britain* CUP (1952)

Eddison, Jill *The World of the Changing Coastline* Faber & Faber (1979)

Fisher, J. & Lockley, R. *Sea Birds* Collins (1959)

Fitter, A. H. (ed) *An Atlas of the Wild Flowers of Britain and Northern Europe* Collins (1978)

Fitter, R. S. R. & Fitter, A. H. *The Wild Flowers of Britain and Northern Europe* Collins (1974)

Fraser, F. G., *British Whales, Dolphins and Porpoises* British Museum (1976)

Freethy, Ron *The Making of the British Countryside* David & Charles (1981)

Gibson-Hill, A. *British Seabirds* Witherby (1947)

Goodden, Robert *British Butterflies: a Field Guide* David & Charles (1978)

Hale, W. G. *Waders* Collins (1980)

Hepburn, Ian *Flowers of the Coast* Collins (1952)

Hewer, H. R. *British Seals* Collins (1974)

Lockley, R. M. *Ocean Wanderers* David & Charles (1974)

Lockley, R. M. *Whales, Dolphins and Porpoises* David & Charles (1979)

195

McMillan, Nora F. *British Shells* Warne (1968)

McGrandle, Leith *The Story of North Sea Oil* Wayland (1975)

Miller, T. G. *Geology and Scenery in Britain* Batsford (1953)

Perry, R. *Watching Sea Birds* Croom Helm (1975)

Richards, Alan J. *British Birds: a Field Guide* David & Charles (1979)

Salisbury, Sir E. J. *Downs and Dunes, their Life and its Environment* Bell (1953)

Sharrock, J. T. R., *The Atlas of Breeding Birds in Britain and Ireland* Poyser (1976)

Sinel, J. *An Outline of the Natural History of our Shores* Swan Sonnenschein (1906)

Vale, E. *Seas and Shores of England* Batsford (1936)

Yonge, C. M. *The Seashore* Collins (1961)

South-Eastern England

The Birds of Kent Kent Ornithological Soc (1981)

Brown, P. E. *Avocets in England* RSPB (1940)

Christy, M. *The Birds of Essex* Chelmsford (1890)

Davis, W. J. *The Birds of Kent* J. & W. Davis (1907)

Gillham, E. H. & Momes, R. C. *The Birds of the North Kent Marshes* London (1950)

Harrison, J. G. *A Wealth of Wildfowl* Andre Deutsch (1967)

Harrison, J. G. *Estuary Saga* Witherby (1953)

Harrison, J. G. *Wildfowl of the North Kent Marshes* WAGBI (1972)

Harrison, J. M. *The Birds of Kent* 2 vols, Witherby (1953)

Jermyn, S. T. *The Flora of Essex* Essex Naturalists (1974)

Manning, S. *The Naturalist in South East England* David & Charles (1974)

Payn, W. H. *The Birds of Suffolk* Barrie (1962)

Ticehurst, C. B. *A History of the Birds of Suffolk* Gurney & Jackson (1932)

Southern England

Arnold, F. H. *Flora of Sussex* Simpkin Marshall (1907)

Beer, T. *Hants & Dorset Birds* James Pike (1975)

Borrer, William *The Birds of Sussex* R. H. Porter (1891)

Cohen, W. *The Birds of Hampshire & Isle of Wight* Oliver & Boyd (1963)

Dixon, C. *Bird Life in a Southern County* W. Scott (1899)

Hales, E. C. M. *Natural History of Sussex* Harvester (1977)

Harrison, J. M. *Bristow and the Hastings Rarity Affair* Butler (1968)

Kelsall, J. E. & Monn, P. W. *The Birds of Hampshire & The Isle of Wight* Witherby (1905)

Knowlton, D. *The Naturalist in Central Southern England* David & Charles (1973)

Phillips, W. W. A. *The Birds & Mammals of Pagham Harbour* Bognor Regis Natural Science Soc (1963)
Whitlock, Ralph *Whitlock's Wessex* Moonraker (1975)
Wooley-Dod, A. H. *Flora of Sussex* London (1937)
Yglesias, D. *The Cry of a Bird* Kimber (1956)

South-West England
Devon Birds The Magazine of the Devon Bird Watching & Preservation Society (Annual)
Beer, T. *Devon's Birds* James Pike (1974)
Burrows, Roger *The Naturalist in Devon and Cornwall* David & Charles (1971)
Darke, T. O. *The Cornish Chough* Bradford Barton (1971)
Darke, T. O. *The Cornish Seabird* Lodsnek Press (1977)
Davis, P. A. *A List of the Birds of Lundy* Lundy Field Society (1954)
Hendy, E. W. *Somerset Birds and some other folk* Eyre (1943)
Kay, Ernest *Isles of Flowers: the Story of the Isles of Scilly* Alvin Redman (1956)
Lousley, J. E. *The Flora of the Isles of Scilly* David & Charles (1971)
Mitchell, J. *The Old Stones of Land's End* Garnstone (1974)
Moore, R. *The Birds of Devon* David & Charles (1969)
Palmer, E. M. & Ballance, D. K. *The Birds of Somerset* Longmans (1968)
Penhallurick, R. D. *Birds of the Cornish Coast* Bradford Barton (1969)
Perry, R. *Lundy, Isle of Puffins* Lindsay Drummond (1946)
Quick, H. M. *Birds of the Scilly Isles* Truro Bookshop (1964)
Rodd, E. H. *The Birds of Cornwall and the Scilly Isles* Trubner (1880)
Ryves, B. H. *Birdlife in Cornwall* Collins (1948)
Scott, Peter *The Eye of the Wind* Hodder (1961)
d'Urban, W. S. M. & Matthews, M. A. *The Birds of Devon* Porter (1892)
White, J. W. *The Flora of Bristol* John White (1912)

Wales
Beer, T. *Welsh Birds* James Pike (1975)
Borrow, George *Wild Wales* (1862)
Chatfield, J. *Welsh Sea Shells* National Museum of Wales (1977)
Condry, W. *The Natural History of Wales* Collins (1981)
Davidson, P. E. *A Study of the Oyster Catcher* (in relation to the fishing of Cockles in the Burry Inlet) South Wales HMSO (1967)
Ferns, P. *The Birds of Gwent* Gwent Ornithological Soc (1977)
Forrest, H. E. *A Handbook to the Vertebrate Fauna of North Wales* Witherby (1919)
Forrest, H. E. *A Vertebrate Fauna of North Wales* Witherby (1909)
Fraser, Maxwell *Introducing West Wales* Methuen (1956)

Handlist of the Birds of Carmarthenshire West Wales Field Society

Jones, W. E. *Natural History of Anglesey* London (1968)

Lockley, R. M. *Letters from Skokholm* Dent (1947)

Lockley, R. M. *The Naturalist in Wales* David & Charles (1970)

Saunders, David *A Guide to the Birds of Wales* Constable (1974)

Wade, A. E. *The Flora of Monmouthshire* Cardiff (1970)

Walker, T. G. *Birds of the Welsh Coast* University of Wales (1956)

The Dee and the Lancashire Coast

Bell, T. H. *The Birds of Cheshire* Sherratt (1962)

Bethell, David *Portrait of Cheshire* Hale (1979)

Boyd, A. W. *The Country Diary of a Cheshire Man* Collins (1946)

Budden, C. W. *The Beauty and Interest of the Wirral* Philip (1921)

Coward, T. A. & Oldham, C. *The Birds of Cheshire* Sherratt (1900)

Coward, T. A. & Oldham, C. *The Vertebrate Fauna of Cheshire and Liverpool Bay* Witherby (1910)

Ellison, Norman *The Wirral Peninsula* Hale (1955)

Hosking, E. *An Eye for a Bird* (chapter on Hilbre Islands) Hutchinson (1970)

Mitchell, F. S. *The Birds of Lancashire* Gurney & Jackson (1892)

Oakes, C. *The Birds of Lancashire* Oliver & Boyd (1953)

Spencer, K. G. *The Status and Distribution of Birds in Lancashire* (1974)

Travis's *Flora of South Lancashire* Liverpool Botanical Soc (1963)

Cumbria and Isle of Man

Allan, D. E. *The Flowering Plants of the Isle of Man* Douglas (1969)

Blezard, E. *The Birds of Lakeland* Carlisle (1898)

Breach, Ian *Windscale Fallout* Penguin (1978)

Carlisle Natural History Soc *Lakeland Ornithology* (1954)

Cullen, J. P. & Slim, D. J. *Birds of the Isle of Man* Manx Museum (1975)

Evans, A. L. *The Naturalist's Lake District* Dalesman (1974)

Garrad, Larch S. *The Naturalist in the Isle of Man* David & Charles (1972)

Hardy, Eric *The Naturalist in Lakeland* David & Charles (1973)

Harris, D. *Cumberland Iron* Bradford Barton (1970)

Hervey, G. A. K. & Barnes, J. A. K. *Natural History of the Lake District* Warne (1970)

Macpherson, *Fauna of Lakeland* David Douglas (1892)

Madoc, H. W. *Bird Life of the Isle of Man* Douglas (1934)

Mitchell, W. R. & Robson, R. W. *Lakeland Birds* Dalesman (1974)

National Environment Research Council *The Sea Bird Wreck in the Irish Sea* (1969)

North West Regional Studies *Flowering Plants and Ferns of Cumbria* Lancaster Univ (1978)

Wheldon, J. A. & Hartley, J. W. *The Manx Sand Dune Flora* Journal of Botany (1914)

Western Scotland and The Isles

The Arran Naturalist Journal of Arran Field Club Vols 1–6
Atkinson, R. *Island Going* Collins (1949)
Booth, C. Gordon *Birds in Islay* Argyll Reproductions (1975)
Booth, C. Gordon *Birds of Jura* Isle of Jura Distillery (1976)
Campbell, M. S. *The Flora of Uig (Lewis)* Buncle (1945)
Cooper, Derek *Hebridean Connection* Routledge (1977)
Darling, F. Fraser *A Naturalist on Rona* Clarendon Press (1939)
Darling, F. Fraser & Boyd, J. Morton *The Highlands and Islands* Collins (1964)
Hardy, Eric *A Guide to the Birds of Scotland* Constable (1978)
Haas, H. *Men and Sharks* Jarrolds (1954)
The Kist: The Magazine of the Natural History and Antiquarian Society of Mid-Argyll
Knowlton, D. *The Naturalist in the Hebrides* David & Charles (1977)
Knowlton, D. *The Naturalist in Scotland* David & Charles (1974)
Lee, John *The Flora of the Clyde Area* John Smith (1943)
MacCulloch, D. B. *The Wondrous Isle of Staffa* Oliver & Boyd (1957)
MacDougall, Lesley *The Crinan Canal* Famerdram Publishers (1978)
Milner, P. *Studies of Nature on the Coast of Arran* Longmans (1894)
Murray, W. H. *The Islands of Western Scotland* Eyre Methuen (1973)
O'Dell, A. C. & Walton, K. *The Highlands & Islands of Scotland* Nelson
Sohel, Arelene *The Western Isles of Scotland* New English Library (1976)
Thompson, F. *St Kilda and Other Hebridean Outliers* David & Charles (1970)
Thompson, F. *The Uists and Barra* David & Charles (1974)
Weir, Tom *Scottish Islands* David & Charles (1976)

North and East Scotland

Bailey, P. *Orkney* David & Charles (1971)
Eggeling, W. J. *The Isle of May* Oliver & Boyd (1960)
Evans, A. G. & Buckley, T. A. *A Vertebrate Fauna of the Shetland Islands* David Douglas (1918)
Fair Isle Observatory Trust *Annual Reports*
Finlay, J. *The Lothians* Collins (1966)
Goodier, R. (ed) *The Natural Environment of Shetland* Nature Conservancy Council (1974)
Goodier, R. (ed) *The Natural Environment of Orkney* Nature Conservancy Council (1975)
Groundwater, W. *Birds and Mammals of Orkney* Kirkwall Press (1974)

Martin, I. H. *The Field Club Flora of the Lothians* Blackwood (1927)

Nicolson, J. R. *Shetland* David & Charles (1974)

Perry, R. *Shetland Sanctuary* Faber & Faber (1948)

Rintoul, L. J. & Baxter, E. V. *A Vertebrate Fauna of Forth* Oliver & Boyd (1935)

Scott-Moncrieff, B. *Scotland's Eastern Coast* Oliver & Boyd (1963)

Venables, L. & U. *Birds and Mammals of Shetland* Oliver & Boyd (1965)

Whittow, J. B. *Geology and Scenery in Scotland* Penguin (1979)

North and Eastern England

Bayldon, J. M. *Guide to the Birds of the Bamburgh Area* H. Hill (1970)

Brady, Frank *The Birds of Berwick-upon-Tweed and District* Privately published (1975)

Chislett, R. *Yorkshire Birds* Brown (1952)

Dickens, R. F. & Mitchell, W. R. *Birdwatching in Yorkshire* Dalesman (1977)

Embleton, Ronald *Birds of the Farnes* Frank Graham (1973)

Ennion, E. A. R. *The House on the Shore. The Story of Monks House Bird Observatory* Methuen (1960)

Gibraltar Point Bird Observatory and Field Station *Annual Report*

Halliday, W. *The Book of Migratory Birds met with on Holy Island and the Northumbrian Coast* John Ousley (1909)

Ingram, J. H. *Companion into North Riding* Methuen (1952)

Morres, A. P. *Among the Birds of the Farne Islands* Salisbury Brown (1896)

Nelson, T. H. and Clarke, W. E. *The Birds of Yorkshire* Brown (1907)

Perry, R. *A Naturalist on Lindisfarne* Lindsay Drummond (1946)

Ridley, Nancy *Portrait of Northumberland* Robert Hale (1964)

Scarborough Field Naturalist Society *Natural History of Scarborough District*: Vol 1 Geology and Botany; Vol 2 Geology

Smith, A. E. & Cornwallis, R. K. *The Birds of Lincolnshire* Lincs Naturalists' Trust (1976)

Spurn Observatory *Annual Report* Yorks Naturalists' Union

Tegner, H. *Natural History of Northumberland and Durham* Graham (1965)

Vaughan, R. *Birds of the Yorkshire Coast* Hendon (1974)

Yorkshire Naturalists' Union *The Naturalists' Yorkshire* Dalesman (1971)

Norfolk–East Anglia

Axell, Herbert E. *Minsmere, Portrait of a Reserve* Hutchinson (1977)

Ellis, E. A. *The Broads* Collins (1965)

Emerson, P. H. *Birds, Beasts and Fishes of the Norfolk Broadland* David Nutt (1895)

Hammond, R. T. W. (ed) *The Broads* Ward Lock (1968)
Manning, S. A. *Nature in East Anglia* World's Work (1976)
Norfolk Bird Reports Norfolk Naturalists' Trust
Patterson, A. H. *Nature in Norfolk* Methuen (1905)
Patterson, A. H. *A Norfolk Naturalist* Methuen (1907)
Patterson, A. H. *Notes of an East Coast Naturalist* Methuen (1904)
Riviere, B. B. *A History of the Birds of Norfolk* Witherby (1930)
Seago, M. O. *Birds of Norfolk* Jarrold (1967)
Tate, P. *East Anglia and its Birds* Witherby (1977)
Turner, E. L. *Bird Watching on Scolt Head* Country Life (1928)
Turner, E. L. *Home Life of Marsh Birds* British Birds (1907)
Wallace, D. & Bagnall-Oakeley, R. P. *Norfolk* Hale (1951)

Acknowledgements

The gestation period of any book is eased by help from many sources and this one is no exception. Carol Pugh prepared the line drawings with great cheerfulness, many photographers allowed their work to be used and Lynette Borrowdaile prepared the map for the gazetteer. My wife Marlene typed the manuscript from what passes for my handwriting and Brian H. Lee spent much of his valuable time checking the proofs.

To all these and to the editorial staff of David and Charles I record my thanks whilst acknowledging any remaining errors to be my own.

Index

203

205